THE ART OF SUCCESSFUL
RESTAURANT SERVICE

THE ART OF SUCCESSFUL RESTAURANT SERVICE

HOW TO MAKE MORE MONEY FOR YOU & THE HOUSE

Give Yourself A 32% Raise Starting Today!

Dan Licitra

iUniverse, Inc.

New York Lincoln Shanghai

The Art of Successful Restaurant Service
HOW TO MAKE MORE MONEY FOR YOU & THE HOUSE

iUniverse books may be ordered through booksellers or by contacting:

iUniverse
2021 Pine Lake Road, Suite 100
Lincoln, NE 68512
www.iuniverse.com
1-800-Authors (1-800-288-4677)

Because of the dynamic nature of the Internet, any Web addresses
or links contained in this book may have changed
since publication and may no longer be valid.

The views expressed in this work are solely those of the author and do not necessarily
reflect the views of the publisher, and the publisher hereby disclaims any responsibility
for them.

ISBN: 978-0-595-46917-8 (pbk)
ISBN: 978-0-595-70631-0 (cloth)
ISBN: 978-0-595-91202-5 (ebk)

Printed in the United States of America

CONTENTS

SALES

Preface

I've written this book as a realistic guide to enable servers to make more money. This is intended for every server (whether you are part-time, full-time, a career restaurant person, working through school or just serving as a side job,) or if you are considering becoming a server in any type of restaurant environment. The methods here have proven themselves true, time after time, without failure. If you want to substantially improve your tips without working more, or work less and make the same money, this book will be of tremendous benefit to you. A 32% raise is the minimum you can expect by reading (and following through with) this book.

No matter where you work, or what type of results you enjoy now, you will profit by reading and applying the principles set forth. They may seem very commonplace on the surface, but isn't success derived from mastering the basics? If you now earn an average of 15% in tips, you will earn 18% to 21%. If you earn 20% now, your goal will be to earn 25% on the average. And no matter what your average tip, you can generate more income by increasing your sales by 10, 20, 30 or even 50%. The math is quite simple. If you're currently making $300 per week, you will be making close to $400 by applying these principles. If you're making $500 per week, you'll soon be earning about $660. **That's an additional $640 per month!** What would you do with this extra money? No matter where you work or what you make, this book will improve your income drastically.

So, while working in restaurants is fun, we don't spend our days and nights interacting with our guests and serving food and drinks just for fun, do we? The goal is to make some money. How much? Well, how much is your time worth? That's the question you need to ask yourself. Because if you work a five or six or eight hour shift at work, you must decide what it's worth for you to be away from your personal pursuits; the very things you work for. My belief is that you should maximize your earnings, every minute of every hour of every shift. That's what this book is all about.

I have been in management for over 20 years and I have been involved with privately-owned restaurants and small corporations, as well as a world-renowned hotel chain with revenues ranging from less than $1 million to over $16 million a year. The biggest allure for me professionally has been the desire to help increase sales and profits for each particular company. Many of the challenges I undertook necessitated building revenues quickly. Tasks included three "start-ups" and several "turn-around." By turn-around, I refer to a business, which is not making budgeted revenues or profits and needs an immediate fix.

These were always, always, accomplished through the development and improvement of service procedures. Elements of the kitchen and menu would also place high on the priority list, but the materials here are dedicated to you; the person in the front of the house that has direct contact with the guests. This is the facet of my career I'm most proud of; working with staffs to create the proper environment in which to grow sales—and do so quickly. So what you are about to read are proven philosophies, which benefit the guests, the company, and you the server. Everybody wins when business is conducted properly. I couldn't have enjoyed any success without people just like you.

I've had the pleasure of working with some remarkably talented people over the years, and with whom I have developed many of the successful techniques you will discover here. This book is a compilation of training pieces I have written to improve their individual success, and increase company sales revenues as a result. By building your success, you generate more and more prosperity for the company and thereby become a more valuable part of the company as a whole.

My success in hospitality is always directly proportionate to my interaction with, and my ability to positively influence, my front line team members. The achievements my personnel have enjoyed (in earning capacity and in promotions) also happen to be my greatest reward and biggest source of passion for me. They are the driving force behind any successful food and beverage operation and their success is what keeps me motivated continuously. Author Sally Koch once said, "Great opportunities to help others seldom comes, but small ones surround us every day." I've tried to live this with my staffs. My appreciation is extended to both my mentors as well as all of the employees I've managed. I have gained invaluable knowledge from both.

Since the core of the restaurant business is, very much, weekend and holiday intensive, it often takes us away from our families, who are the people we're working for in the first place. I can't tell you how many people I've worked with (including myself) who have sacrificed precious time away from their kids and significant others in order to bring home a paycheck. Time they can never get back. Our kids have one childhood and if we're too busy trying to earn a living, we miss out on a portion or most of their young lives. The reason I have stayed in this business so long is because of the pleasure I have found in helping others succeed.

The sole intention of this book is to allow you to be more successful at your job during the time you're already there. I don't want you working anymore, just more productively. This way, you will spend less time there and more with your family, with more money to enjoy doing the things you love to do. There're only so many games, plays and recitals before our children grow up and move out on their own. My children are coming up on their 14th and 16th birthdays respectively and I know I've missed more than I should have. So I am both empathetic and sympathetic to your current work schedule.

I will illustrate that *the way* in which you do things will enormously impact your take-home pay. By changing your methods and your focus slightly, you will be able to realize a significant improvement in your take-home money each week. My goal is to get you to a point where these actions are automatic and require little effort over time. As a result, your actions will help improve the business of your company overall. Your contributions will be substantial enough to drive revenues up.

The other benefit you may experience is your ability to train other staff members. Managers want everyone to increase sales and prosper. The more quickly you grasp this concept, the more valuable you will become to your restaurant. Nine out of ten salaried employees started out as hourly employees, according to the National Restaurant Association. So you may place yourself in consideration for management down the road, if you so desire.

In the Beginning

If there is one resounding theme in this book, it is to "Be Brilliant at the Basics!" This is where success comes from in the restaurant business. It is simply the result of executing certain steps and creating a fun, comfortable atmosphere for your guests. The restaurant business is *very lucrative* when you concentrate on the fundamentals. And the best part is, there are ways to dramatically increase your income very quickly. You can realistically increase your monthly income by 50% or more without working an extra day by working smarter, not harder!

Any amount of success in our lives comes from the repetition of a skill. The more we read, hear or see something, the more it's placed in the forefront of our thoughts or concentration. The more we concentrate or focus on something, the better we get at it. As a server, it comes down to two basic skills—1) Establishing a rapport with your guests, and 2) selling food and drinks. If you put your attention on those two things, you will see marked improvement in your tips immediately. And your increased sales will add to your restaurant's bottom line.

Both you and your owners want the same thing: to increase sales in the restaurant. Your owners also *want you to earn more tips* because this means the guests who frequent the restaurant are leaving happy and satisfied, which means they will be back to patronize the restaurant again and again (hence the term, guest frequency). Your guests want good food and good service. And they will spend more, as a result, when you provide those things. It will put a lot more money in your pocket, as well as add to the company profits.

You also place yourself in the enviable position of being assigned the good parties and the VIP reservations. *You know*, those parties who spend *and* tip the most. Don't the managers and owners put the best servers, the ones who sell the most, who guests ask for the most, on the most important parties? I know I do. That's what this book is about; getting you to elevate your performance through some very simple processes that will soon become second nature to you.

The following pages are dedicated to the philosophy of great service and developing an instant connection or bond with your guests. It's meant to illustrate very plainly how you can increase your income working in this business, or how to succeed if you wish to enter it. It simply describes the truisms of the business and how to work intelligently and use your personality. The goal of this book is to describe how you can work exactly the same amount of time you do now, not harder or more often and still make more money. Most everything applies to bartenders as well as servers, but for ease of writing I will simply refer to servers.

You will find that *focusing* your thoughts will benefit you immensely. To create success in anything, you must consciously direct your consistent actions. In order to improve any aspect of your life, including this portion of your professional life, you must focus on what you do consistently to enable you to achieve the best results. Those who have difficult earning money in this business are not focused on the basics. They tend to forget, get lazy, or stop looking at things from a guest's point of view. So this book is meant to serve as a tool and a reminder of the many things you already know, but sometimes forget when you're going through the rigors of your daily shift.

This book will show you how to make more money, without serving a single guest more; without working a "double" or unscheduled holidays, or even picking up a single extra shift. In fact, you won't have to work one extra hour! How much more can you make? It's all relative. Once, I worked with a bartender named Sandy who focused on the very things you will read here, and she ended up driving a $60,000 Mercedes in less than a year! It just happened to be her dream and by focusing on a few distinct points, she achieved her goal in an extraordinarily rapid fashion.

Her income rose immediately and by the third month, she increased her tips by over $800 per month (which was the car payment I believe). And she is only one example. I can tell you about people whose earnings as servers helped them take one or two great vacations per year, or buy homes for themselves and their families. The list goes on and on.

If all this sounds a bit extreme, or more in line with what you might hear in an overnight infomercial, consider this very carefully because numbers speak the truth. You have in your power the ability to give yourself a 32% raise beginning today. I don't know of many other people who have as much ability or control over their raises, but you do. As you read on, you will find all the information you need contained in these pages, but this is how it essentially works.

By increasing your sales a mere 10%, and adding only 3% more to your tips average (let's say from 15% to 18%), you will at the end of the day, week and month find approximately 32% more money in your pocket! If your average customer's check is $15, I'm going to show you how to almost effortlessly make it $16.50. Not much right—$1.50 (or 10%)? And just by being a little more pleasant and attentive, which is illustrated in numerous ways in this book; you will easily bring your tips up a modest 3%. Then

you will have given yourself a more significant raise than most anyone could ever hope for. YOU control this, not your boss. This book shows how to accomplish this more easily than you ever thought.

What you will learn, or simply recall, is how *we* like to be treated when we go out to eat. All those little nuances that make one's dining experience so much better. It's noteworthy to remember that a big pitfall in the restaurant business is that the same things are performed so often and so repetitively that they sometimes become trivial in nature or are forgotten. When this happens, if we don't realize immediately, our service will be inferior and our income will reflect this instantly. Remember, ours is an instant gratification business or instantly non-gratifying if we fail to execute the proper service.

The reading of this book will be easy and quick. You will probably nod your head while reading portions of this book because certain information you know already. But like any other skill, we must be reminded and continue to improve all the time. It's when we "settle" or think things are "okay" that we see a decline in our professional life. I am of the belief that we either ascend or descend, but we never remain in the same place for too long. If you feel like things are good enough, I promise you, your performance will quickly decay. Things are really never good enough because we can always improve what we do. Whether it's timing, presentation or sales skills, the further we develop all of these factors, the more money we put in our pockets.

There are only three facets I'm going to elaborate on: Attitude, Performance and Sales. These are the things that really drive our earning capacity. They are at the core of what we do. Service techniques and other particulars in this business are company specific. After all, you might work for the Ritz Carlton or a family owned luncheonette and they each have their ways, which are appropriate for their respective environments. I do not wish to contradict them. This book will simply enhance your skills in order to make the most of your time spent at work.

Now no matter where you work, you will have people that don't tip the common standard of 15% or those who will only tip 15%, no matter how awesome you are. But for the 80+ percent of people who do tip according to service, these practices will assure you of earning much more money.

As you begin to apply the concepts in this book, you will eventually incorporate these ideas with little or no effort. That's the best part. I don't want any of this to be complicated. We all know if things are too hard, we'll probably not stay with them very long, and figure either we failed, or the information was bad. That's the last thing I want. This is going to be easier for you than you can imagine. It will take some focus in the beginning, but you will also see results very quickly, which has a way of keeping us motivated, doesn't it?

ATTITUDE

"Success is not the key to happiness. Happiness is the key to success. If you love what you are doing, you will be successful".
—Herman Cain

YOU ARE THE FACE OF YOUR COMPANY

Generally speaking, for you to be successful, your company needs to be as well, and vice versa. At least if you're looking for the long term. So, it stands to reason that the better our efforts make our company, the better and more abundant success we will all realize.

Not only are each of our individual actions critical to the results we enjoy on a daily basis, but so too for that of the company we represent. And make no mistake, a customer coming to your restaurant for the first time, will judge the organization by *your* actions. Your manners, courtesy, promptness, professionalism and quality service will comprise much of how the entire business is perceived.

According to industry surveys, 73% of the reason customers return to a restaurant is service!

Now I don't mean to say that the food isn't a determining factor in the customer's opinion of your location. It is. But for our purposes, we will assume that all the food is of good quality because you can't control that completely. Later I'll describe in more detail, steps you can take to create some quality control here, as well, in "Service Hints."

A guest will make many determinations about your company based on *your* performance. They will form opinions on your company's hiring practices, ability and commitment to training, your principles when it comes to everything from your minimum acceptable qualifications of employees to your neatness of attire. Your appearance, demeanor and every action you take will be a direct reflection on your company. This includes your personality because it is, or should be, a large component of the hiring checklist in this business.

These clues, which a customer receives from you, paint a total picture about the company. This is where the value of trust comes into play concerning a company. Do you want to do business with a company you don't trust? Who does? This then goes to questions of character and integrity regarding the company. If you stop and really think about it, as consumers, you make all sorts of quick judgments and rationalizations based on your observations of sometimes the smallest of details. And even if you are incorrect, it still becomes solidified in your mind as to what you consider good and bad. And which companies are deserving of your business.

Aren't people's actions and reactions based on their moods too? You have probably seen people who criticize, complain or badmouth something or somebody when something else totally unrelated is bothering them? Not you or I of course, but we do know people like this, right?

Your guests are no different. If these clues form a negative feeling about the company, what guest is going to want to return? That's why it's imperative we do not give any reason for a consumer to make these types of snap judgments. The better the impression you make, the more confidence the guest will feel about your company, and as a result, this will help retain and attract new guests all the time. This is so critical, and yet is often an overlooked aspect of your significance in your role.

Even if you wish to leave the company out of this equation, don't you want the guests to have the best opinion of you personally? For this reason, you need to be certain you are paying attention to every aspect of your look, attitude, duties and always portraying a positive image for both yourself and the company. Put your best foot forward and make that great impression, and even the most critical of customers will recognize your effort and commitment to service. This is the beginning of success.

THE GREETING

Your relationship with your guests begins with the greeting—when your guests are seated. You are first judged on how long it takes you to approach your guests. That's right, your guests could be angry at you *before* you ever even see them! **Nobody likes to wait**. This can cost you a portion of your tip later on, so take notice. Even if you're incredibly busy, pass the table, say hello quickly (but don't seem rushed) and let the guests know you will be right with them. At least you have acknowledged them. You may even ask a team member to take a drink order so they are "occupied" for a few moments.

When you do engage your guests, your first exchange, facial expression, tonality, body language, eye contact can be worth 10% more or less in your tip. **This is not an exaggeration.** How you first set the tone for your guests will in their minds, determine what their experience is going to be like the entire night with you as their server. "You only get one chance to make a first impression" was a hugely successful commercial slogan for a brand of shampoo.

Allow me to paint two different pictures for you to better describe what I mean. For example, we have two servers, Kevin and Darlene. If you have dined out, you have most likely experienced both of these scenarios I am about to describe. Let's say you're a party of six; three couples on a Friday night. Kevin is our server. He comes over to the table after about five minutes with barely a smile, a look of frustration across his face, slumped over a bit, head more down than up, talking in a low voice with little or no energy, or even a desire to be there. Everyone looks around the table and is thinking the exact same thing without ever saying a word. Kevin has already set the tone for the experience his guests will have this night. Kevin's first words are "Does anybody want anything from the bar"? Now this probably won't ruin your night out, but didn't it feel like a little air came out of a balloon? "Why is this guy even a waiter?" someone usually asks. Or sarcastically, "this guy's gonna to be a lot of fun.".

Now think of the opposite possibility. Two minutes later, Darlene approaches the table. She welcomes you and your guests warmly and sincerely with a smile, introduces herself in a pleasant tone and in those brief few seconds, has made eye contact with every single person sitting at the table (which is huge because eye contact is a sign of acknowledgement and we all like to be acknowledged). Darlene hands out a wine list and asks if the group would like a cocktail while looking over the menus, and even suggests a couple specialty drinks. She knows you're out to have a good time and wants to help make that happen for you. Now you and your guests are a little more upbeat and ready to have some fun because this is the tone Darlene set.

Now it's important to note that table approaches are dependent in part by *who* it is you're approaching. You will speak and act a bit differently if your guests are four business men, rather than a mother and father with young children, or perhaps five ladies who may be a bit older. You need to be a bit more reserved in different situations, but smiling and appearing pleasant are constants.

Now here is the key: Kevin and Darlene did the same amount of work and spent the same amount of time with their guests and yet achieved two very different results. And that's what I mean when I say that working harder is not what makes you earn more money in this business. If you set a bad tone, no matter what you do the rest of the night, you have created a negative perception about yourself, and in part, your restaurant. People come out, in part, to be entertained. You are a part of that entertainment. How entertaining was Kevin?

Conversely, Darlene has made the initial impression a favorable one, which accomplishes three critical things.

1) Assuming 15% is the standard tip, Darlene has already brought herself up to a 20–25% tip with her demeanor, as long as she is able to perform her duties, naturally.

2) Now that Darlene has established a bit of a rapport, she is in a better position to offer suggestions with acceptance from her guests. These "suggestions" are one of the ways in which Darlene will add value to the guests' experience, and increase her sales and subsequent tips.

3) Since we already have a liking for Darlene, she has earned herself some latitude if everything is not perfect, or if the food takes an extra few minutes. She has built up some goodwill with us already. Because we tend to forgive people we like, don't we? You create a host of benefits for yourself in the first minute of serving your guests. I cannot stress this enough.

As a server, you must go to the table anyway. Why not serve in a productive manner that benefit you, your guests and the house? Look again at the three things Darlene did accomplish and realize all of the things Kevin did not accomplish. All Darlene did was act pleasant and upbeat; happy to be there. What a concept! If you're not happy while you're serving tables, do your guests, coworkers, owners and yourself a favor … find a new line of work. There is no job worth any amount of money (I never thought I'd say that) if you're unhappy. There are tons of jobs, which require no contact with people. Find one. Being with people is the absolute best part of the restaurant business to me and should be to you, if you want success.

Showbiz

It's funny how closely the restaurant business resembles show business. Depending upon what setting you find yourself in, whether you are in a hotel, fine or casual dining restaurant or some trendy bar or nightclub, you might find yourself in front of hundreds of people per day. You're always on stage; the better you perform, the more money you make. Maybe that's why so many aspiring actors dabble in the business while waiting for their big break. It allows you to hone your skills and get comfortable in front of people. Maybe not, but serving certainly is closer to acting than most other lines of work.

I have worked with part-time actors and models that have lacked traditional service skills, but excelled when it came to the sheer presence they exuded in front of their guests. It's a huge positive if one is an extrovert, although I've known many people who were not but could play the part well. Their guests would compliment them and ask for them specifically when they came to the restaurant.

We're always performing. The key is inviting people to like you. We do this with our actions and personality, just like the example in the greeting section. When people like you, the difference in your tips is staggering. Until you get into luxury hotels, exclusive or truly fine dining settings where things are clearly more regimented, you will be judged, in great measure, by your personality. I'm not trying to say someone who's incompetent can make up for this with some attractive behavioral traits. They can't. Or that being a server is as easy as being nice. You still have to execute. But a lesser amount of skill can be compensated with a great attitude. And great service skills are truly magnified when coupled with incredible personal qualities.

There is obviously more to serving besides your smile. Just as in acting, serving is all based on timing and attention to every detail. You must focus yourself every day, during every shift on your "Steps of Service" so you can properly coordinate all things to ensure your guests' satisfaction. Imagine watching a play where an actor forgets a line, or times one incorrectly. What would your reaction be? It's no different than if we omit or forget to do something. The same bad results occur. If you've seen the production before, you'll know it immediately and will probably have a very critical reaction. Even if it's your first viewing, you will sense something is wrong. You will do well to remember, your audience has dined out before, so they also look for certain things. They know what they like and what to expect.

To divert from this often leads to disappointment on the viewer's part. We are expected to act in a certain manner while properly serving our guests so as not to disappoint them. The part we play in the restaurant business is that of a happy, enthusiastic, energetic individual. There are variations to this, but that's what makes the individuality of a good server unlike that of any other. We've all had experiences where certain aspects of a person stuck with us and invariably had a positive impact. But it's certain that it was always derived from an optimistic, upbeat nature.

Those qualifications are a must. I have worked with people who had little or no experience and still became great servers because they had the right mental and emotional makeup for this business. The reverse is also true. I've seen servers who were more talented than most would ever hope to be, yet had no flair and their lack of solid earnings showed that. Their abilities could never quite compensate for their inability to establish a rapport with their guests at the table.

You must never underestimate your role in the guests' experience. You're on stage every time you step in front of a table or serve at your bar. Yes, they come out to eat and drink, but their needs and desires extend past simply getting a drink or a bite to eat. This could all be done at home. You can certainly add in convenience, as well, but most enjoy the human connection; the interaction or entertainment factor. The personal touch is crucial. It's all part of the dining experience. The more you give, the more you get. Don't be afraid to engage in conversation and banter with guest, as long as you read people well to determine what type of interaction they want. Stand out and be noticed.

I know this is a huge generalization, and I don't mean to suggest the kitchen operation in a restaurant is insignificant by any means. I have had the pleasure of working with some extremely talented chefs and cooks. And, after all, we all want better food than we can make ourselves at home. But for the purpose of discussing the front of the house operation, let us assume that essentially a steak is a steak is a steak. If this is the case, the difference becomes the ambience; the service and the feeling one gets while in a certain atmosphere. I can think of a dozen places, near my home, where I can order a steak I will truly enjoy. Fifty percent of these eating establishments all share a similar ambience and décor. But two or three of the twelve have the best servers. And I don't mean that of the Four Seasons, but just really cool, pleasant people who always go out of their way to make sure you're well satisfied. Remember the 73% reason?

Great service can usually make up for mediocre food. However, great food can never make up for poor service. This is because a good server can be sure you enjoy yourselves by providing those "intangibles" and creating a pleasant experience. Have you ever been to a restaurant and, at the conclusion of the night, said to yourself, "The next time I go out to this restaurant, I am going to be sure and ask for that particular server"? That server made such an impression that it just wouldn't be the same without them. That's the memory we often take away with us when we've enjoyed ourselves. And, that's what your guests will soon think of you, if they don't already. Can you see now your significance and the control you really have over the guests' experience? It makes all the difference in the world!

CREATE THOSE "FEELINGS" FOR YOUR GUESTS

In the restaurant business we sell food. But we also sell a "feeling." This feeling, in particular, depends upon the establishment for which we work. It could be of elegance, a party atmosphere, country charm or a number of others. There must be a feeling in addition to food and drink. And you are largely responsible for creating those feelings.

Advertising firms will create ads and commercials that depict their client's restaurant chains in a very precise manner. Just think about any of the restaurants you see in commercials. Everyone is smiling, laughing, joking and having a great time. Because this is what the ad agencies want you to believe about these companies. This is the way you're going to feel if you eat at (such and such). They'll show food and drinks too, but have you ever seen a commercial for a restaurant with two people sitting at a table having a serious conversation? And, truth be told, we do go out sometimes for a quiet romantic dinner, or to have a serious conversation or business meeting. But we want to know where all the fun is when we're going out to be social.

If you work in a place that has more than one dining area, think about this for a moment If a guest has a choice to sit in an area where there are people and things going on, or in a section that has no one else seated in it or nothing going on, where does the guest most often ask to sit? If they're out for a social reason, it will be the busier area. That's because we like action. That's what drives people to busy places because they want to be where everyone else is. Don't friends try to get friends to go out to the busy, cool, happening places where you'll see everyone, and everyone will see you?

The advertising executives are depicting this setting as one of great fun and excitement. That's part of the restaurant experience. The *feelings you* will experience when you go there. Please don't ever underestimate the importance of this. I've been to restaurants whose food was outstanding, but it was boring. Now you don't need to act like a circus performer, but just understand that part of our business is making sure our guests enjoy the feeling they hoped to find.

There's a casino close to me that has great commercials. I take notice as soon as I hear the music on the television. It shows couples and friends, dining, drinking, dancing, celebrating, cheering, all set with a background of excitement, glamour, music and winning money. What a fantastic place this is, you think to yourself! I want to get in my car and go there as soon as I see it. It's incredibly effective because it conjures up all the things you want when you go out. It creates this image that you just have to be a part of.

Now if you've ever gone to a casino before, you know what you see does not always depict all that's going on there. In fact, the guy that just lost half his paycheck isn't doing the tango with his wife in the parking lot while they wait to give the valet the last $5 they have left, so he can go find their car. But you know what? Even that man will get those good feelings back after a little time passes because, in reality, we want to have fun and enjoy ourselves. And we're willing to overlook some things to feel this way.

I worked with a woman named Kim for a few years. Kim would always make her customers feel so incredibly welcome and comfortable, the minute they sat at her table. She would also be very engaging to all of the tables next to hers. She knew the value of the guests' feelings and would use this talent to earn close to 28% tips on average! I would have to remind her many times about certain service points, but her guests loved her.

Above & Beyond

"Going above and beyond" to serve our customers or "exceeding expectations" are common catch phrases in any service industry today. And, I suppose that these things mean different things to different people. What these statements mean to me, and hopefully to you, are doing more than your guest anticipate. It's the "wow" factor that successful businesses of all types provide for their customers. And I don't mean bringing out a bottle of ketchup with a customers French fry order, so the guest doesn't have to ask for it. That's expected. Or delivering a straw with a drink. What I do mean is doing something that your guests will talk about to their friends. Perhaps getting a fussy child to smile a little so her parents can enjoy their dinner. Or making a really big deal over someone's birthday or anniversary. Or getting the cooks to make something special for your guest because their diet doesn't allow many choices.

I was once a guest at the Renaissance Vinoy Resort in Tampa, Florida. I stayed there for five days. The hotel was very pretty. You could feel the elegance the second you pulled up to the front entryway. But this story has nothing to do with the hotel's décor. I've been in many hotels, some of which were perhaps more stylish or luxurious. I enjoyed the food I ate at each one of them, but nothing else really stands out. The pool areas were always clean and the grounds were always well manicured. But what does stick out in my mind, what I will always remember about the Renaissance is their staff. From the valet standing in the entrance to the front desk, to the bellmen, the housekeeping and the restaurant staff, they couldn't do enough for you. You could walk through any part of the hotel, at any time, and every single employee would make eye contact with you and greet you with some pleasantry. Each and every one provided a warm, sincere greeting that made me feel quite comfortable and at home. My wife was not with me because it was a business trip (which she is kind enough to remind me about from time to time) and I remember the first thing I told her about on the phone was how extraordinary the staff was there.

Being in this business, I am usually the last one to ask for anything extra or out of the ordinary because I hate to impose. I did however want to send my wife something for her birthday, which took place during this trip, other than flowers. The woman at the front desk couldn't do enough to help me find the perfect gift. She emailed me five different websites with unique gifts to pick from in my room. There was no way she needed to do this, but she did. She was such a pleasure to deal with. The rest of the staff was also polite, attentive and always cheerful. The impression will last with me always.

Guests also appreciate this attitude when they make other, perhaps more unusual requests. I can't tell you how many times a guest has come into my restaurant long after the kitchen had closed. I could have told them in my nicest, most polite, sincere voice that there was nothing I could do to help them. But the minute they entered our doors, they were my guest (even before they spent a dime) and I thought it was proper for me to offer them a few items I could make for them.

Their reaction and appreciation far exceeded the extra little effort it took on my part. And sometimes they become a customer for life. People appreciate your extra effort.

When I was younger and very inexperienced, I was overseeing a large function for a local politician in our city. It was a cold night and therefore the coatroom was filled beyond capacity. I noticed a man wandering around with his coat and asked him if he would like to set it down. He said yes, but the coatroom was filled and he didn't want to leave it unattended. I asked if he would like me to place it near where I was working so I could watch it for him. He turned out to be the husband of the person who had organized the event. At the conclusion of the event, he introduced me to his wife who thanked me for my small gesture and assured me I would see them again. This wonderful lady booked probably 50 more functions with me worth hundreds of thousands of dollars over the next several years. All for just a little extra effort.

Unfortunately service is not a priority with every company. Just visit a mall someday. While most stores have a well trained staff, we've all walked into places where the staff either ran or hid, or acted like they were doing you a favor by helping you or they just ignored you. That's why little extra kindnesses are so very well appreciated today. We're so used to poor service in certain situations that it makes good service more noticeable. You always have to be a little more attentive towards the good referrals because those customers may be with you for a very long time.

So the next time a guest asks you if you could bring her half blue cheese and half ranch on her salad, instead of sighing and reluctantly agreeing, try saying "absolutely, we can do anything" and smile. You'll be amazed at the results. Get your guests to enjoy themselves far more than they ever thought they would. Do not give good service, but give great service. There is great quote from Charles Kendall Adams, who was president of Cornell and the University of Wisconsin which reads "No one ever attains very eminent success by simply doing what is required of him; it is the amount and excellence of what is over and above the required that determines the greatness of ultimate distinction".

WE CAN DO ANYTHING

People are going to have different likes, requests and even needs. Just assume this going into your customer exchange. Our job is to be as accommodating to our guests as possible. Is there anything worse than asking for something and having a person look at you as if you were out of your mind, like "How dare he ask me for that" type look?

Anybody can say no, that's easy. In fact, as customers we are sometimes afraid to ask for certain things, which may be an inconvenience. It's like we've been conditioned to accept this type behavior. I know my wife won't say anything or ask for something she thinks might be inconvenient. How did we get to the point where we've become intimidated to ask a store clerk, cashier or server for additional help? This is even more of a reason for you to go out of your way. Imagine how much this will make you stand out!

Once, I was having lunch with a friend who wanted a simple grilled cheese. It wasn't on the menu, but there were items that consisted of bread and cheese, so I know it was possible. However, the server's response was "I'm sorry, that's not on the menu." Knowing this was probably the result of the kitchen staff and not her, I asked if the chef wanted me to explain how to make a grilled cheese sandwich. Rude I know, but it was completely incomprehensible how this could be said to any guest.

Now I will admit that some things are out of a server's control, especially when it comes to food in the kitchen. And I'll bet this was one of those times. But that's when you need to see a manager so your guest can get whatever they want. If you have the products in-house, it should never be an issue. That's what we're here for; to take care of our guests better than anyone else could. This creates gratitude, which breeds loyalty and results in return customers again and again.

I've worked on several occasions with a chef named Patrick. Now I realize that his is a "back of house" position rather than a front of house, like yours. I merely want to illustrate customer service for a moment. Patrick has no formal culinary training and, as a result, does not know how to make everything, and possesses no knowledge of desserts or pastries. But he does have one thing that many people lack and that is the desire to do anything to try and please a guest. And if you have ever watched him running a pasta, carving or omelet station on a brunch, you would see him be one of the most charming and engaging people there is in the business.

One time, I remember one frequent guest came in and wanted an omelet with spinach. The server, who was waiting on the guest, said they would even be willing take frozen spinach. Patrick however, would never settle for less when it came to the guest. He left the two other cooks there and drove down the street to pick up a bag of fresh spinach, ensuring the guest's overwhelming satisfaction. I think you can safely assume that this act covers "Above and Beyond" and "We Can Do Anything" all at once. There was no limit to what this man would do and, wherever he goes, he is always an incredible asset. I should know, I have the good fortune of working with him again, 25 years after we first worked together.

Keep this in mind. Most people aren't aware of how easy, or difficult most requests are. So if you can do it with a "We Can Do Anything" attitude and a smile, you will endear yourself to these guests. So much good can come out of fulfilling what is quite often a small request. All the guests really know is that you didn't tell them "No." In fact, denying a guest's request should only be used as a last resort.

Sometimes we need to be creative about how to accomplish a guest's request, but it will always be worth it in the end and pay exceptional dividends. Strive to do half of what Patrick did and you'll never go wrong. Think of ways to say "yes" before you ever say "no." Your customers' gratitude will not only enhance the perception of your restaurant, but also put more money in your pocket.

Teamwork

(If you want the job done right, you can't do it yourself)

The fact that this section follows "We Can Do Anything" is no accident. The "we" in our business is crucial. Most everything described in this book is about what *you* can do to improve *your* earnings. But it's important to mention, we're all dependent on each other. A team is defined as any workplace group with a common goal and ownership of shared responsibilities in achieving that goal. Our common goal is to create great experiences for our guests so they will return again and again.

We can only do so much on our own. Any operation will run better and more efficiently when everyone involved cooperates. You know yourself, that if the people in the back of the house (chef, cooks, prep people, dishwashers, etc.) don't work well with the front of house staff (servers, bartenders, bussers, etc.), you're not going to get anything done, and your business will suffer greatly.

The most obvious example I like to illustrate to my staff is when you're passing another server's table and the guest tries to get your attention. So many servers respond by telling the guest they will get their server for them. So they need to go find the server, have the server go all the way back to the table, go back to get whatever it was that the guest wanted and return again to the table. It is insane to waste this much time and effort.

The original server passing should politely have asked what the guest needed and responded to it themselves. If this server is so busy that he or she has no time, he could have at least told the original table server what the guest's need was so that server could handle the problem without having to walk all the way back to the table.

It's simply a matter of efficiency. All customers in a restaurant are our guests, and that must show in our actions. Please don't ever, ever take the attitude that "It's not my table" and disregard a request. By doing so, you will be creating such a negative perception that even though you may not feel any negative ramifications that night (as a reflection of your tips), you certainly will not too far down the road, just in business alone. Every action and every word of yours affects the business your company can and will do.

Even from just an appearance perspective, if the staff is not working together, it can cause a tension in the room that can befall upon your guests. It creates a very uneasy feeling. Nothing is better than watching a staff that works well together. We're no different than any sports team. We don't compete against each other, only other restaurants. On the other hand, I do believe positive, competitive scenarios can be set up between staff members to add a little fun and excitement to a restaurant. Contests are a great way to foster a productive atmosphere that drives everyone's performance up, but never to the extent that you are working "against" one another.

Your staff should exercise the same philosophy that any other team would. And in order to do this, you will all need to work together. If you work together to make your establishment a success, not only will there be enough money for everyone there, but actually more because of the cumulative effect the teamwork will have on your prosperity. And your focus on teamwork will go a long way in optimizing your success.

PASSION

Passion exists in all areas of our lives: spiritual, emotional, mental and physical. We need this energy in our professional lives as well to realize our purpose and goals. You need to develop your passion because it is everything in our business! Those who have it stand out from the masses. There's a certain attractive quality that comes from this emotion and draws people to us. It can also turn a challenge into a tremendous opportunity. Passion also provides an air of confidence to those who possess it.

There must always be an excitement and enthusiasm present in the way we go about our job. Courtesy and politeness are key characteristics, as well, but you need to infuse a bit of eagerness in addition. There's nothing worse than having a server take care of your table when they look and act like they would rather be anywhere else on the planet. And I'm not suggesting anything difficult or more labor intensive, just a slightly different mindset.

If you only go through the motions, even if your serving skills are outstanding, you will leave the guests with a feeling that they missed a certain something. We need to have an obsession with making the guests' experience the best it can be. We should want everyone at our tables to really enjoy it and remember us to the point where they recommend us when they talk about our restaurant, and ask for us by name when they return.

Like a great salesperson, we are always trying to not only make the sale today, but to line up future business. This is where great servers become great earners. And it all starts with passion. Think of your position as your own business, without the start up expense or overhead. If you make the right impression, people will return and ask for you. If you're not getting people to come back and see you, you're losing out on the biggest tips.

People who are impressed with you, and return to see you, will already be better tippers than most. Why? We've already gone over it. Because they like you! People will always do more when they like you. But first, you have to do more for them in order to deserve their gratitude. You need to make *them* feel like they are important to you! Make *them* the center of attention. We all want to feel that way. Don't forget, everything begins with you and your actions.

Portray an Attitude of Gratitude

Servers who think they deserve a tip before they do anything are doomed to failure, or at best, a mediocre earning capacity. Just because society somehow says that tips should be 15%, we sometimes think we are entitled to this money. We're not. I'm amazed at a server who does a mediocre or poor job and gets upset about the lack of tip. "They didn't even leave me 15%," they blurt out. That's because you didn't deserve it. You need to earn it all the time.

The cornerstone of our very business is how we make another person feel. In the last section I talked about the way you make your guests feel. How many times have you gone out and felt like you were an inconvenience rather than a valued customer. It happens in retail stores, movie theaters and professional offices, as well as eating establishments. **Make your guests feel appreciated from the start**. Let him or her know that you're happy and grateful that they chose your restaurant to dine in today.

Everything in life is give and take. From the moment we meet someone, a tone is set depending upon the first exchange. If person #1 approaches person #2 in a kind, friendly manner, #2 will usually respond in the same way. This is how life works, so naturally our professional relationships (between our guests and ourselves) are merely an extension of this law. Call it karma, if you will, but we generally get back what we send out. So let's not give our guests any reason to be defensive or put-off by our actions or mannerisms.

If you begin to look towards your guests with a gracious, thankful manner, right from the start, your outward actions will automatically reflect this attitude and the response you receive from your guests will follow suit. Act as if they have already given you a great tip. Anticipate (not expect) the feeling and you will feel differently about your tables right from the start. When we "expect" something, this usually means we feel we're entitled to it, while anticipating is equated more with looking forward to something, or thinking something is likely to happen because of our actions.

As a result of this way of thinking, you will find that you will begin to demonstrate a greater passion and enthusiasm for your job. In fact, you may just find yourself enjoying this thing we call "work" because your outlook has changed. Sometimes the chain of events that occurs when we make small changes in our lives ends up creating a much greater impact than we ever imagined. You will also find that your tips will increase immensely as a result, which will make you happier and more appreciative, and so on, and so on. Just get the cycle started in motion and nature will help things along naturally.

"You simply will not be the same person two months from now after consciously giving thanks each day for the abundance that exists in your life. And you will have set in motion an ancient spiritual law: the more you have and are grateful for, the more will be given you".
Sarah Ban Breathnach, Simple Abundance

The following is an excerpt from a study I found interesting and noteworthy:

Highlights from the Research Project on Gratitude and Thankfulness

Dimensions and Perspectives of Gratitude Co-Investigators: Robert A. Emmons, University of California, Davis; Michael E. McCullough, University of Miami

Well-Being: Grateful people report higher levels of positive emotions, life satisfaction, vitality, optimism and lower levels of depression and stress. Their disposition toward gratitude appears to enhance pleasant feelings while diminishing unpleasant emotions. Grateful people do not deny or ignore the negative aspects of life.

EXPECT SUCCESS

Henry Ford once said, "If you think you can, or if you think you can't, you're right." As trite as this lesson may sound, many people convince themselves everyday, before or on the way to work, whether or not it's going to be a good or lousy day. And they are always right, as a result. In general, your thoughts determine your actions that then determine your experiences in life.

Now I'm not suggesting that if we walk around all day saying how great life is, we'll somehow hit the lottery. But I am suggesting that what you expect, you eventually receive. Please don't confuse "expecting" with "dreaming about," not that you can't realize your dreams. But you have to create a plan to attain them. Sitting in your bedroom just hoping will do nothing. Remember I mentioned the woman, Sandy, who bought a Mercedes in less than a year? That was originally only a dream.

The difference is she made it reality by working towards the goal of increasing her earnings to be able to afford it. She did something about it. What's your dream? Is it a car, a great vacation, or money to go to school? Is it a condo on the beach, a little house in the suburbs? You'll see in a later section of this book, how to clearly and specifically do these things yourself.

Success is a way of thinking, acting, preparing and doing that changes everything. The ultimate objective of success, in the restaurant business, is delivering great value to the guest. When we accomplish this, our guest wins, and that means, we ultimately win. In working with any of my staffs, I always expect each and every one of them to succeed, no matter what their skill level is. More often than not, partly because of these expectations, my staff members do succeed.

People tend to live up to, or down to, what is expected of them, by others and by themselves. If you expect good results from yourself, you will eventually realize them. The famous poet and novelist Johann Wolfgang von Goethe said, "Treat people as if they were what they ought to be, and you help them to become what they are capable of being." Here's your chance to set the bar for yourself, so set it high. My father used to tell me that you should shoot for the moon in life. He said that even if you miss, you'll still be among the stars.

In our business, it's fundamentally necessary that we believe we will succeed every time we step on the floor or behind the bar. If we feel like we're an average server, then our actions will prove that out as will our tips at the end of the day. There's a thin line between confidence and arrogance, but you need to walk that line and believe in yourself whole-heartedly and without question.

You must first think like a pro. This alone will elevate your performance. When we feel we're as good, if not better than the other person in our business (including those we answer to), our minds will begin to believe it over time and this will become our reality. With some minor exceptions, YOU are the one who determines the quality of your life, which includes your professional performance and the amount of money you earn. It's okay to anticipate a great tip, as long as your skills and style make the guest feel like you deserve it. We get what we expect in life. Just like if you say to yourself in the morning, "this is going to be a bad day," it usually will end up that way. Just like every great athlete who competes expects to win. They condition their minds to believe it and, no matter what anyone else does, it cannot and will not affect their performance. If your mind expects something, it will do all it can and move you in that direction, which in the case of serving will focus you on your duties.

I worked with a server named Dan who would tell you before the night started that he would earn more than anyone else did. And he was right more than not. And it was his personality more then his serving skills that made this happen. He was confident and created such a great experience for his guests that he would, more often than not, earn more in tips than his colleagues. I think he actually enjoyed the idea of simply making more, than the actual money itself. He was an ordinary guy, with an extraordinary sense of taking care of his guests. His guests would always comment on how charming he was. He did favorably because he got everyone to like him. And he earned a lot of money!

I have, and always will, made considerations for people who want to be servers, have no experience, but have great attitudes. Sometimes it actually works out better in the long run because they do not bring along any bad habits, or deeply imbedded beliefs from another company which are not conducive to the way I or my company may want things done. It's a sense one gets when interviewing. If you ask the right questions, you can oftentimes determine the chances of this person succeeding.

I really enjoy training individuals on the types of philosophies you're reading now. That's why I am so confident that this book will truly enhance your earning capacity no matter what your current skill level. Anyone can learn to take an order, set a table and carry food. You need the ability to make positive impressions on people; to really care about what you're doing.

If you give the guest what they want (a great experience), they will give you what you want (a bigger tip). This is the basis for every single successful sales transaction. And, this is a very simple exchange. Your guests will part with their money for the goods and services you provide; food, service and those *feelings*. That's what they're buying. And if they part with their money, but we don't live up to our end of the bargain, they will return no more. Plain and Simple. So create those "feelings" and make sure your guests enjoy. Anticipate that great tip and your service will begin to warrant it. When your guests leave, you can trust they will be back.

Keys to Success

As in any successful company, in most any industry, the employees are the foundation and the core essential of the business. You become the "face" of your company and the way in which guests perceive the operation. Keep the following in mind as little reminders for specific points:

- Always be prompt and punctual for your shift: To ensure that you are completely prepared to carry out your duties, and not to inconvenience your fellow associates, remember, **"Early is on time, on time is late and late is unacceptable"**

- Practice teamwork and respect your fellow employees: By looking out for one another, you are better able to serve your guests. Be courteous, at all times, to your fellow associates and resolve any differences at the appropriate time, and in the appropriate place. Pitch in anytime, anywhere, in order to make the guests' experience the best it can be.

- Take ownership of your position: Be creative within the company guidelines and don't be afraid to suggest ideas to improve things. The worst thing we could ever feel or say is "*This is good enough.*"

- Take pride in the facility: It is everyone's responsibility to report problems or defects in equipment. It is also everyone's responsibility to keep your facility clean for your guests.

- Greet every guest no matter how long they have been in your building: Make eye contact, smile and say hello. Conduct yourself in a professional manner at all times. Do not use slang with the guests and always remain pleasant.

- Listen to your guests and offer suggestions to assist them: Don't get huffy when a guest offers a constructive criticism. Welcome feedback, whether positive or negative, this will help you learn, grow and improve yourself and the company.

- We all make money based on selling products and services to our guests, but we are not "salesmen": Remember, people love to buy, but hate to be **sold** something. Be subtle, suggest, educate, inform and ask questions. These methods will generate sales and not offend people, bringing the guest back again and again.

- Be knowledgeable: Familiarize yourself with as much of the operations possible. This will allow serving your guests better and enhancing their experience. Ask for training, if you are not sure about any aspects of the operation.

- Try to accommodate every request: Your job is to accommodate as many requests as possible while keeping within company and moral guidelines. Think of creative ways to say "yes" to your guests.

- Be Personable: This means to always be warm, friendly, charming and helpful to the guests. Pay complete attention when conversing with guests and give them your total attention. Make each and every person feel as if they are special to you and your restaurant.

- Show a guest to a restroom or coatroom rather than pointing: Even if you take three or four steps with them, then extend an arm towards the destination, this will create a much nicer sense of service to your guest.

- When replying to a guest's expression of thank you rather than using the standard "you're welcome" or "no problem," try using **"my pleasure."** This creates a warmer, more service-oriented feeling for the quest.

- Always thank every guest as they leave your restaurant: It doesn't matter if they were at your table or not. Always smile and provide a sincere thank you, in order to make the guest feel appreciated on the way out. It is the final touch for the guest's overall experience with you.

Performance

"Excellence is to do a common thing in an uncommon way."
—Booker T. Washington

COMMUNICATING TO
YOUR GUESTS

Wherever you work, a POS system is hopefully in place by which you are to serve your tables. I will try to stay away from specifics, in order keep everything in general terms so as not to contradict the guidelines set forth by your company. There are points that translate into any company's system, so this is meant as a reminder or just a slightly different slant on procedures.

We'll begin with what is most paramount in our business. Communicating with our guests heads the list. There are so many subtleties to this that it is essential we cover this in detail. As we interact with our customers, please remember that the majority of our messages are conveyed non-verbally. Remember the example of the two servers greeting the table earlier? Guests will pick up on all sorts of things before you even open your mouth. According to sales and marketing experts, this is how people receive messages:

- 55% through body language and gestures

- 38% is tonality and voice inflection

- 7% are the actual words we use

This is huge. Please re-read these numbers again because this affects all aspects of everything we do and the significance of this needs to be fully grasped. Isn't it amazing that *what* we actually say to someone is given the least amount of attention? What is critical is the way we portray ourselves through our facial expressions, posture, hand gestures, the way in which we walk and simply stand. Our message is communicated and conveyed far more by our enthusiasm and mannerisms than mere words. You can portray a warm and sincere attitude, or one that more likely says, "I just want to get through this as quickly as possible." You can have several people utter the exact same phrase and it will mean something slightly, or even drastically, different each time by the way they deliver the message. Body language and tonality always seems to create an underlying message if we're not careful.

Attitude is infectious and drives behavior. Your **attitude** is the first thing people pick up on when it comes to face-to-face communication. Just as laughing, yawning, and crying are infectious, attitude is as well. Before you say a word, your attitude can influence people and influence them into taking on your same behavior. Somehow just by looking or sensing, you can be infected by another person's attitude, and *vice versa*.

Attitudes drive behavior in another way. Your **body language** is a result of your mental attitude. By choosing your attitude, you acquire a mood that sends out messages everyone understands, consciously or unconsciously.

What you are shouts so loudly in my ears I cannot hear what you say.
—Ralph Waldo Emerson

The most important thing in communication is to hear what isn't being said.
—Peter Drucker

Always make eye contact when speaking to, or listening to, a guest. It's not only a sign of respect and politeness, but also an indication of your self-confidence and composure. You're also giving the guest a feeling that they are all that counts right now! This is one of those little extra touches that are so often overlooked in our business these days.

Think about people who talk to you and don't look at you when you're speaking with them in a store or restaurant. They are either distracted, thinking about something else or just not very interested in what you have to say. Is anything more annoying when you're patronizing a business, which is supposed to revolve around service?

We need to always be sure to smile and make the guests feel welcome. Greet every guest the first time you see them, no matter how long they have been in your building. I can never figure out why so many servers look away from guests as they pass them enroot to the bar or kitchen. Saying hello takes no effort at all and is very welcoming to your guests. Here's a good rule of thumb: **Make eye contact with guests at 10 feet away and say Good Morning (Afternoon, Evening) at 3 feet (acknowledge everyone within 5 feet of you).**

Is there anything worse than going into an establishment to spend your hard earned money, and feeling like the employees couldn't care less if you were there or not? Or worse, like you were an inconvenience? This happens all too often. And most of the time the servers never say a word, right? It's the look on their face, or the lowering of their heads or some other abstract gesture. I'm sure most of the time, this is unintentional, but, nonetheless, this employee has not made you feel very appreciated.

Be on the lookout for guests who may have a question or need assistance. Oftentimes, in restaurants, people feel funny or embarrassed about asking a question, maybe about an item on the menu that they are not sure of, especially if the menu items are in another language. No one likes to appear foolish or less knowledgeable than the rest of their group. Make sure to read their facial expressions and see if you can offer them assistance in a way that makes them feel comfortable. Be proactive. If you see a guest that appears to need something, ask! Sometimes it's as easy as standing next to the person, while addressing the group. This allows the individual to quietly ask you, or even point to the item on the menu for clarification from you.

Never use slang in front of your guests. Even if you're in a casual setting and have a table of young men and women, don't approach and say, "Hi guys." They're not guys and you risk offending the women. It also suggests a certain familiarity with the group that may seem inappropriate. Avoid words like "how ya' doin", "yeah', "nope" and "hang on." I'm not suggesting you address them with, "Good afternoon ladies and gentlemen," but with a simple, "Good afternoon," to the group works best. When it's a table of just men or just women, then use the gender. You can be friendly while remaining professional.

Remember to always let the guest know what you "Can Do" first, rather than what you can't. When you simply say no to a guest's request, it creates a sense that you don't want to cooperate. No body likes to be told no. Remember the grilled cheese scenario? Its little things like that, that cause you to lose your tip money, and for the house to lose a repeat customer. We can do a lot more than we sometimes think. So, always be conscious of trying not to disappoint your guests if this can be helped.

While your guests are eating, be sure to always check back to be certain they are satisfied. Believe it or not (and I know this is hard too)

96% of people who are dissatisfied will not complain, even if they're dissatisfied. Ask specific questions. Rather than, "Is everything okay"? Try, "Is your steak cooked to your liking"? Look for signs, even if they say everything is okay. Like if they are eating slowly or not at all. The other major way you can communicate with guests is by being visible. Once you have verbally checked on your table and you're continually passing by, monitor the need for additional drinks. Simply be in sight and glance at the people at your tables. If your guests need you, they will signal. If you're in the back somewhere, you'll never know and not be caring for the guests properly.

The final thing you want to communicate to your guests is a sincere, "Thank You," for coming and to invite them back again. We all want to be appreciated. Even after a perfect experience, the thank you is like the cherry on top of the sundae. And when a guest thanks you for something, reply with "My Pleasure" or "Your Welcome." Don't ever use "no problem," because when you say this, subliminally it reads like something or someone was a problem. Remember, they are your guests until they walk out the door.

Anticipate Your Guests' Needs

There is a myth in the service business that claims, "we should be there when our guests need us. The fact is, we should be there before, and in anticipation of our guests' needs all the time. We need to foresee the next set of occurrences, so we are not always in a reactive mode. This is Proactive Customer Service.

The perfect example of being *reactive* is a server who is content when they are present for the guest to re-order a drink. If we were doing our job properly, we should have asked the guest if they would like an additional drink *before* the guest asks for it. This is not only good service, but this will increase your check total and average cover. It makes such a difference when a person is dining out and the server is there before he or she is called for. This shows the server is are paying attention and focusing on the customer, which reinforces a sense that the customer's business is appreciated. I never, ever consider this over selling or being pushy. This is simply excellent service.

If a guest has to request more water or bread or butter or more coffee, the server/busser is not doing their job. You must be more than an "order taker". You must develop an instinct to know what your guest needs, before they do. That's taking care of the guest. "Are you ready for another bottle of wine"? This is not only good service, but also great for sales. The two most often will go hand in hand. Let's say you have six tables one night and half of them turn you down. You still sold 3 extra bottles of wine, and if they cost $30, you just added between $13 to $18 to your tips that night.

Now maybe you say, "Big deal, thirteen dollars." If you do this consistently, multiply it by 4 shifts per week, by 4 weeks per month. That's $208 per month extra for you. And we've only mentioned one item. Do this with all the options the guest has and really multiply your income.

Even if you pick up an extra drink on every table you wait on, watch the increase in total sales for you for that night. And we're still only talking one drink per table. You will see how often we have an opportunity to sell something, just because we were standing there. You can't do it when you're talking to your co-workers in the station. I promise you, that is one spot you will never make any sales.

Just take some time and study the people at your tables. It's not hard to develop this sense because you will find people are fairly predictable. You say, "That's too hard, I can't read people like that." Okay. Just think about yourself sitting in the chair and what you would be thinking about, or want next or desire. Use your own experience and tastes as a guide. This will eventually become very easy and make you much more productive in your sales and service.

CLEANLINESS

Your venue must be clean from the minute the guest hits the parking lot. Now, while that will probably not be your responsibility, the inside of the restaurant is. And there are specific items and places that need to be looked at before every shift. Is there anything worse than sitting down at a table that's dirty or surrounded by debris?

Be proud of your restaurant's appearance, just as if your family or the owner were going to sit in your station. Floors and carpets should be clean with a vacuum or broom. In addition, you should try to maintain cleanliness throughout the shift (as in not stepping over debris each time you pass it). Chairs need to always be wiped so as not to have a guest see any debris as they are seated. Tabletops are obvious: Salt and peppershakers should be filled and clean to both the sight and touch. Same thing applies to your sugar caddies (whether they are kept on the tables or brought with coffee service). Any trim around the walls or booths should be dust and debris-free. Tray stands and all trays should be clean. No one wants to see their food come out on a dirty tray, even if it's not directly touching it.

Any wait stations in view (or otherwise) should always be kept neat and orderly. Any windows or glass (not to suggest you go clean all the restaurant windows) which have any food, hand or fingerprints that can be easily wiped off, should be.

Not only are these things health issues, but people lose their appetites or feel less pleasant and uncomfortable when they are surrounded by "unclean" areas. This all reflects on the establishment and you as the server. How many times have you seen a coworker walk over a crumpled up napkin instead of reaching down to pick it up? Everyone needs to be conscious of these things.

And please, please wipe all the silverware and check for spots on your glasses. Sometimes the machines don't get everything as clean as we'd like, so we must be diligent in our observations.

Personal Appearance

The truth is, we do judge a book by its cover. This is so very important because this clearly makes a statement about you and the business you work for. I know each restaurant will have their own specific rules regarding everything from jewelry and hair to tattoos and fingernails, but let us put a few basic rules of thumb out there.

Please start with your uniform. It needs to be cleaned and pressed every time you work. Don't go to work with wrinkled pants or shirt. It's untidy and gives the impression that you don't care. Guests and fellow associates are entitled to expect a general cleanliness from you, as you are from them. This may sound elementary or even ridiculous, but I have seen employees who did not bathe, shower or brush their teeth before coming to work. Needless to say, this is not a pretty sight. Do not wear excessive perfume or cologne. Hands should always be impeccably clean. Nails should be trimmed and clean.

Females: Nail length should be kept moderate. If you wear nail polish, please keep fully polished or none at all (do not leave nail polish chipped or half worn off). Cosmetics should be used in moderation and appropriate for the setting and time of day. Hair should be clean and neatly combed. Hair should not fall into your face or obstruct eye contact with others. Variations on hairstyles that project something other than professional appearance should not be worn in the workplace

Males: Properly trimmed moustaches and beards may be permitted where you work, however, daily stubble is not attractive. Hair must be clean, neatly combed, free of excess oils and gels and tied back if longer than collar length. Hair should not fall into your face or obstruct eye contact with others.

Phone Etiquette

Always use proper telephone etiquette. This is a huge reflection on your company's reputation as well as the employees. It sets the tone for what a guest can expect when they dine with you. Poor manners on the phone have cost countless restaurants too many reservations. Say, "Good morning", "good afternoon", "good evening", and then, "Thank you for calling (company). This is (your name)." Answer in a pleasant, upbeat voice and smile while you are talking. Believe it or not, smiling is noticeable on the caller's part. Always ask permission to place them on hold or transfer their call.

Now, you probably thinking, "How is this going to help me increase my tips?" While it won't instantly, all of these suggestions for improvement will in the long run because you'll impress potential clients and help attract them to your restaurant. A server is a sales and marketing person as well. It's the little things in our business that separate us from the competition. You are always an ambassador for your company, so be proud and represent your company professionally at all times.

Service Hints

1. Service is the very fiber of our business: **We are in the service industry.** The rules are simply—Places with poor services go out of business, places with good service survive, and the places with outstanding service prosper and grow.

2. Your mission is **"to meet and exceed the expectations of your guests:"** Outstanding service can not be compromised at all. Don't ever say, "It's Good Enough." The second you say that, your guests will begin to suffer.

3. If we do not properly prepare for each shift, we will fail without question. There is nothing worse than scrambling around trying to get ready while our guests are walking in to be served. It is of the utmost importance that this part of our day is not taken for granted or overlooked. By the time our first guest enters, we should be completely finished and ready to greet our tables!

4. Assist other servers when your tables are okay. TEAMWORK is a key to success. If a guest from another server's section asks for something, try to take care of it on your own rather than going to get the server to find out what they need. This will save time and be more efficient. We are all responsible for the happiness of each

and every guest ... this means even the ones not sitting at our tables.

5. Devote yourself to the needs of your guests from the **time they enter** the restaurant until the **time they leave**. Greet them quickly and warmly with a smile. Serve them with all the skills and personality for which you have been chosen.

6. Anticipate your customer's needs. Guests should never be made to wait. Customers should NEVER have to wave frantically to attract your attention. If you think you're doing a great job because you were there when the guest asked you for more bread or more water, think again. You need to anticipate that and tend to it before you are asked. That's good service.

7. Keep your tables as clean as possible AT ALL TIMES. PRE-BUS at all times.

8. You should be in your station with a clear vision of your tables, and within sight of your guests unless you are picking up food or drinks. Your guests should be able to get your attention easily if necessary. Please avoid being the server that asks you every five minutes if everything is fine. Once you have served a course, you naturally want to check to be sure the food is all cooked properly. After that, simply pass by your tables and make eye contact without uttering a word. If your guests need you, they will ask for you.

9. Answer customer's questions courteously and briefly. We are here everyday so what may sound like common sense to us, is not to our guests.

10. Have two recommendations of appetizers and entrees that you like and can suggest, in case the guest is unsure. Always ask the guests

what they would like for an appetizer. If they seem reluctant, suggest splitting an appetizer. Give them something to think about while you're getting their drink orders.

11. When taking orders do not ask yes or no questions (choices).
Ex. would anyone like a cocktail from the bar?
Incorrect

   Ex. Would you care for a cocktail or a glass of wine to start?
   Correct

   Have a couple of specialty drinks that you like to recommend to guests. Have knowledge of your premium wines to "up sell" to guests. For non-alcohol drinkers sell non-alcoholic frozen drinks, bottled water, etc. as opposed to a soda for instance.

12. Always take cocktail re-orders on glasses 2/3 empty. Sell, Sell, Sell! This is going to help you tremendously in increasing your average covers.

13. Always anticipate your next step in service, getting accompaniments or additional service pieces on the table prior to needing it. Consolidate your trips to the kitchen.

14. Check Your Food Before You Serve It. Anyone who has worked in this business for even a short period of time will tell you that sometimes a member of the kitchen staff will get careless and send something out that is not correct or up to company standards. Do not serve anything to your guests that you would not serve to a family member of yours. I don't care if you have to get a manager (because the cook is telling you to take it out anyway) to correct the problem. Don't settle on the quality or presentation of your guests' food ever. You may not make it, but you are the final set of

eyes that determines whether or not it's worthy of going out to the table.

15. Always check back on food within two minutes of serving an order that you can correct any problems or concerns immediately. Remove food from dining room immediately, if dissatisfied—DO NOT TALK ABOUT IT IN THE DINING ROOM AND NEVER DISPUTE A GUEST—REMOVE THE PLATE. Notify Manager. If the guest says everything is "fine" and is not eating the food on his or her plate, everything is NOT FINE. Be curious, find out what the problem is, and notify the manager immediately no matter how small you think the problem is.

16. Take special care of children at the table. You don't need to hang all over them, but a little extra attention goes a long way with parents, and you should also try to get their food out to them as quickly as possible. This way they don't get fidgety at the table.

17. Always offer dessert, coffee/specialty coffees and after dinner drinks (increase your check average). Show the dessert tray when available, or at least recommend a dessert or two that you especially like (remember, servers are salespeople).

18. Before you total a check, make sure it is accurate. Deliver the check only when the guest asks for it. When you take cash, please don't ever ask the guest if "they need change". It can be offensive to many people, especially if they have a $30 check and have put a $100 bill in the check book. Just bring back the change, no matter the amount. The guest will never leave you less because you brought it all back.

19. We all work together and must practice TEAMWORK at all times. It's worth repeating. We are all dependant upon each other to create the type of atmosphere that will promote our individual successes.

20. Always give a gracious and appreciative good bye to your guests and thank them for coming. You also want to invite them back to come see you again. Don't let the guest leave without letting him know how important he or she is to you.

CRITIQUE YOURSELF

Your owners, managers and coworkers are certain to give you suggestions and criticisms regarding your abilities and performance. Listen always, because even if you learn one thing out of every ten suggestions, you will be better off than before. Remember, we all learn from everybody, no matter what their position is or how much their educated or how long they've worked there. Please don't ever stop learning or improving your skills.

You need to also develop the habit of reviewing your own performance in order to determine what you did well and worked, and also what you could have done differently which may have provided better results for you. You should also be asking yourself what things felt comfortable and which did not. Many of the things you incorporate into your serving "style" naturally need to fit your personality. What works for one, may not necessarily work for another, and that's okay. Find out what works for you.

Create a sheet that you can fill out after your shift that acts like a journal. Fill it out as accurately as possible and mark your progress by reviewing it prior to your next shift. Store your journals by the month or the day of the week. You might also want to arrange them by the shift you've worked (breakfast, lunch dinner, etc.). This is also an excellent tool for cocktail servers or those who work in bars and clubs. Because now you're bottom line comparison is how many guests, and how much in liquor sales.

If your company uses a POS (point of sales) computer, most of the information you need to keep accurate records will be on your server report. Look at the following as a possible template for yourself. This is one way to accurately and tangibly measure your results and progression on a daily basis. It may take you a couple of extra minutes at shift's end, but I promise you that it will not be an inconvenience. You will actually begin to look forward to this part of managing your business. Every business owner looks at the bottom line daily. You're no different. Watch your bottom-line and it will pay dividends to you.

While this may seem simplistic or unnecessary, the difference in your sales when you become focused on and more aware of your daily results is amazing. If you actively do nothing else, please do this because it will improve your sales. It is a powerful tool for obtaining success! Just by the mere fact that these numbers are now consciously part of your thought process, you will see quick results. You can't help but improve just by the sheer fact of placing your attention on the numbers.

Our business is a game of numbers. Even the best servers don't always make their 21% or 25% tips on every table. But when they get an 18% tip on one, you can bet that they will get a 25% or 30% tip on the next to balance it out. That's the bottom line. Don't let one mediocre or even bad tip throw you. What counts is at the end of the day and the end of the week. What's your average? Remember there will be people who dine with you on fixed incomes who, as much as they may like you and be pleased with your service, cannot afford a generous tip.

Look kindly upon them and never with disdain. What goes around comes around. Treat them just as nice.

Performing Well is the Best Advertising in the World

You can find an unlimited amount of books describing specific marketing techniques that will drive customers to your restaurant. Many are sound and deserve consideration. Prior to considering any of them, you need to very clearly understand that THE EXPERIENCE YOUR GUEST HAS determines whether you will succeed or fail. The most brilliant marketing minds in the world cannot save a restaurant that does not take care of their guests.

Control what occurs within the walls of your restaurant, and create the best guest experience you can. This is the first step of successful marketing. And if you do everything you can, to the best of your abilities within those walls, you will be successful. The advertising and marketing of any truly good restaurant is done by their customers. Word of mouth can make or break a business. You can never hope to buy a newspaper or magazine ad, or a radio or television spot that has the power of an enthusiastic customer recommendation. It just doesn't exist.

By satisfying your guests, you put salespeople on the street for you everyday. Don't you tell people about a great experience while out having lunch or dinner? We all do. And with more enthusiasm because we experienced it first hand. In describing your tale, doesn't it always end with, "you have to try this place!" You just did for that restaurant what no ad ever could have.

It's true that advertising and marketing companies, spend billions of dollars a year to get us to do this, buy that, go here or stay there. And the good ads certainly make us respond. But isn't this always more convincing, more believable and has a greater impact when someone provides a testimonial? Doesn't this, more than any other marketing material, cause a greater sense of urgency on our part to get there?

Your good or poor performance will be talked about at offices, clubs, on trains, at school and anywhere else people meet each other. Are you more likely to try a new restaurant because of a recommendation from a friend or from looking in a phone book? Every guest that leaves your table is now a walking ad for your restaurant, good or bad.

And bad stories are told almost twice as often as good. This is important to remember. We tend to forget how we talk about our recent experiences. Our customers talk just as much and just as loud. So let's get them to talk positively about our location. And if you do your job really well, they'll be talking about you specifically as well. This, in turn, will result in future customers we haven't met yet.

Advertising is used by even successful companies to help keep their names in the public's mind. But restaurants who don't conduct business quite as well as they should, spend much more of their revenues trying to attract or get back customers. Oftentimes in the tens of thousands of dollars per year, this money could be going to other things, like employee incentives and bonuses. This may be your money being spent on all of those ads.

Even if you are of the opinion that you don't care what your boss spends in advertising, consider this: Because the advertising you generate through your customers by offering great service, this is, by far, more convincing than any newspaper or radio ever could be. This will bring **you** new customers much more quickly, which translates into more tips in your pocket. Let your customers be your marketing professionals. They do it better and more effectively than any paid promotion could ever possibly hope to. Remember, it starts with you though.

First, you need to demonstrate your commitment on a daily basis. You need to dedicate yourself (and your company) to constant improvement (better, faster, different, etc.). The biggest enemy in this business is complacency. This will destroy business faster than mediocre food ever will. This alone will hurt revenues, lose jobs and close restaurants.

- * **Remember 96% of dissatisfied customers don't complain.**
- * **90% of those, if they have a choice, will go elsewhere.**
- * **They will usually tell 9 other people about their bad experience.**
- * **People who have a good experience usually tell 5 people.**

SALES

"People become really quite remarkable when they start thinking
that they can do things. When they believe in themselves, they
have the first secret of success".
Author unknown

How to Give Yourself a Raise by Generating More Tips

Many of us in the hospitality business fall into a pattern of believing we need more guests to make more money. The truth is, while we always want to attract more guests, we can substantially increase our sales without increasing the number of people we serve. As a result, our income increases right along with it. In fact, if you didn't wait on one single guest more, you can still substantially increase your income.

I've worked in places where even on slow nights, certain people still made good money. Perhaps they prepare themselves a little more, knowing on a Monday for instance, it's not going to be as busy as a weekend. Maybe it's because they spend some extra time with their guests because they can afford to do so because there are less tables in the restaurant. The truth is, good servers earn all the time, no matter what the conditions are. The difference between good earners and bad ones is *what* they think about when business is slow.

By this, what I mean is that you can tell yourself on a Monday, for instance, that it's going to be slow tonight and I'm going to try and get out of here as soon as I can. While their counterpart is saying, since I'm only going to have a few tables tonight, this will allow me time to really take care of my guests. Consequently, while most servers are leaving with $20 or $30 in tips for the night, the good earner is walking away with $60 or $80 on a slow night (figures are relative for this example). Sometimes success in life comes not from having the right cards, but from playing bad ones properly.

If another server is complaining that they need more guests to earn more money, most often they're making excuses for their own lack of effort, performance and focus. It's easier for them to blame something or someone else for their difficulties. Take care of who you have right now. If you do this, more people will naturally follow and your current customers will come back more often.

BE ABLE TO SUGGEST WITH CONFIDENCE

Suggesting with confidence, you will see, when we get to the tip charts, is going to be crucial. It starts with knowing your menus, food and cocktails, in great detail. What I always suggest to servers is to pick two or three cocktails (and do it according to season or climate, like using frozen drinks in the summer or warm climate places), two appetizers and two entrees. You should not only have seen them, but have tasted them so you can be sincere in your recommendations.

People, especially those who come to your restaurant for the first time, will often look for suggestions to avoid being disappointed by ordering something they're not sure if they will like. The better prepared you are ("Fail to prepare, and you prepare to fail"), the more easily and quickly you can assist the guest. You can also lead them to items that may be a dollar or two, or three, etc. more than some others to bring up your average cover.

When you suggest something to a friend or an acquaintance, are you nervous or afraid they will reject you? Not usually, right? Have you ever told someone about a dentist or doctor that you're extremely happy with? Have you ever suggested a brand of shampoo or a place to buy clothes? We all do, and most everyday, and with success many times. In fact, if you have that much success when it comes to persuading your guests to take your suggestions, you're already way ahead of the game.

Why do people take the suggestions we offer? For two reasons: One, is they have a need or a desire. Two, you come across as very convincing when you describe the product or service. You describe it with confidence and conviction, like you are doing them a favor by giving them this valuable information. You believe in what you're saying, and this comes through. Aren't you just as confident in several of your menu items and specialties? If so, the transition is easy. If not, find a better place to work, where you can be proud and confident of your menus.

Remember this too: most people who go to restaurants do so because they want to buy!!! Do not forget this. Even the people, who go out and count pennies, **want** to buy. Even when we're broke, we want to buy. It's our nature to spend. Your customers just need a reason from you, along with perceived value so they don't get that feeling of "buyer's remorse." Don't be intimidated. Don't take a "no" personally. You already have a thicker skin than many or you wouldn't have chosen this business.

THE SUBTLE ART OF
SUGGESTIVE SELLING

Even though we don't consider ourselves to be salespeople, we are. Don't be turned off by this because it may instantly conjure up thoughts of a slick talking, less than ethical type salesman. The proper way to conduct a sale is to be certain both parties benefit. Get the picture of the telemarketers out of your head. You're not "cold calling" someone. They are there to buy. They are there to spend money. All you need to do is help them in their decision-making to get the most out of their experience.

You already sell things (or suggest things as in the previous section). In our everyday lives, we sell. We sell our ideas, thoughts and beliefs and opinions to our family, children, friends and co-workers, most of the time without ever realizing it. With great passion, we're able to describe television shows, books, movies, salons, music and stores that we try to get others to experience as well. We even try to persuade strangers, at times, if our convictions are strong enough. So why shouldn't we approach our jobs in this manner when it will clearly benefit us financially?

The best part is, in our business we can be much more subtle with our guests than we are with the people we're closest to. As a result, our "selling" simply becomes "suggesting." And, after all, who knows your restaurant better than you? If you go to a store and ask for help, don't you pay attention to, and often take the advice of, the person working there? Of course, we all do. They must know what they're talking about, we think to ourselves.

Part of helping our guests enjoy their experience is guiding them through the ordering process at times. People have come here to eat and drink. Ninety percent of your work is already done because they're not browsing. You think suggesting in your environment is hard, try retail sales someday. That would really make you appreciate what rejection feels like.

But, the restaurant business is different. People come and sit at your table with money out to buy some of the items on your menu. So, suggesting cocktails, wines, appetizers, entrees and desserts is one way of assisting them. If you're knowledgeable and speak confidently, people will listen and follow your recommendations. Plant your feet and speak clearly, with confidence and sincerity. People also love to try new things when they go out. That's the best part about going out. No one wants the same old thing. This is why consumers are open to you suggesting specialty drinks and appetizers, entrees and desserts. I will oftentimes ask my server for recommendations when eating at a restaurant in which I've never been to before. Hotel restaurant workers should excel here because of all the transient clientele. You should be recommending your head off! If you work in a hotel, or really in any area that attracts tourists and visitors, you have a captive audience. Use it to your benefit.

You will find people in our business that do not believe in selling to the guests because they feel its offensive. I respectfully and humbly submit they're wrong. We do sell things. The difference is you are not going to come across as a salesperson. That's what makes the difference. You can accomplish this without being disingenuous. It simply comes down to the fashion in which you communicate to your guests. Two people can say the exact same words, yet have two very different meanings. The first key is your delivery. The second is to be certain you are adding value. People will spend extra as long as they receive extra value.

Think about this for a minute. Every business tries to sell more of their products and services. The people in McDonalds try to get you to *super size* your meal, or at least ask you if you want fries or a soda with your burger—Every Time—and with tremendous success I might add. They are simply "up selling." Do you get offended? Of course not. Is this person a better communicator than you? Are they smarter or do they possess more business savvy? You tell me.

Go to any post office in the country today and mail a package. All of the staff members there are instructed to ask every customer (in addition to what he or she is already doing) if they are in need of any stamps or supplies today. This is their form of "up selling." All successful companies do it. That is their way of conducting business. The customer's perception is merely determined by *the way* in which it's done.

Just follow the first rule of selling: Be Gentle, Be Kind. People don't like to be sold. But people love to buy. Buying implies control. Being sold, the opposite. That's why we never force, we tempt. This always gives the final say to the guest, who is still in control. All you are doing is providing an enticing and appealing description of a few of your favorite or best products. You are simply creating a more attractive and persuasive portrayal than any mere wording on a menu could. You're creating a verbal picture that teases his or her desires. In real life, if you really wanted a friend to buy a piece of cake, you'd probably start by describing how great it smells, how gooey it is and how thick the frosting is, and how it will melt in his or her mouth. Appeal to your guest's emotions in order to induce action. People always buy more on emotion than logic.

The Do's & Don'ts on Cocktail Service

I wanted to address this portion of your sales in particular, because I feel it's where servers run into the issue of being pushy the most. It's one of those things that can be perceived as manipulative by the guest. We need to be sure we don't offend anyone, so be a little more conscious during this interaction.

When a guest orders a vodka and soda from us, one direction to go in is to ask them if they want ABC brand. Half of the people will say that's fine or the bar brand is okay, but half will say something like, "If I wanted ABC, I would have asked for it" in a less than kind way and with a disgruntled look.

That's because this can sound like we are just trying to increase the bill without providing any extra value, especially to someone who does not consume alcohol all that often. They feel that vodka is vodka, so don't try and sell me the more expensive one. My suggestion to my staff is always this: When a guest orders vodka with no name attached (or gin, rum, scotch, whiskey, tequila or bourbon), simply ask them what brand they would prefer. Now, you're merely trying to find something to their liking without the suggestion of a more expensive item in their mind.

You will get three reactions to this very unassuming question:

1. I'll take ABC.

2. Bar will be fine.

3. What do you have?

If they answer number 1, you effortlessly made the sale. If they answer number 2, you have gotten your answer without offending your guest. Prepare yourself for number 3 by knowing a couple name brands in each category. You must answer quickly and with confidence, and you will get the up sell easily. At least you have a two out of three chance for an up sell. If you avoid this problem, you have eliminated the most common error, and one of the most distasteful to your guest.

Opportunities for increasing cocktail averages will also arise when people ask you about specialty drinks you make, including frozen, martinis, margaritas, etc. Your biggest prospect in food or liquor, however, lies within your wine list. More and more people today are turning to wine as an alternative to hard liquor drinks because of several factors including driving safety. Many people also have a real interest or passion in wines. Wine tastings are very common and a lot of fun. Wine clubs are becoming as popular as book clubs among many people.

Here's one of those opportunities where your product knowledge can make or break you. You will find everybody from the novice to the connoisseur, and every person in between ordering and drinking wine. You need to be a little savvy here. I don't want to try and turn this into a wine course, which could keep you reading for hundreds of pages. But there are some basics and I think you will find you can request that your manager set up a short wine seminar for the staff through the companies your restaurant purchases wine from. They can go into some more detail about wines, tastes & flavors, descriptions and even the regions in which they originate.

When it comes to wine, you need to find a couple to recommend in addition to your house wines. Normally you'll have a Cabernet, Merlot, Chardonnay, White Zinfandel and Pinot Grigio for your house pours. Today many restaurants have stepped up the amount of house pours to include Zinfandel, Shiraz, Cabernet-Merlot blends, Chianti, Fume Blanc, and so on. You need to know at least one, if not two, in each category, that you can suggest. Wines and their flavors differ tremendously—much more than liquors and, as a result, many people really enjoy indulging in new wines all the time. There is also more of a perceived value with wines.

It is actually a very educational process to many. So this is a great place to up sell while adding tremendous value for your guest. Prices may vary by as much as $2 to $12 per glass between house and premium wines. Think in terms of a table of four guests ordering premium wines and adding maybe $32 extra to the check—each round! If you are in a restaurant where you have a decent wine list, you may find yourself in a position to sell bottles that range in price from high teens to the 40's, 50's and 60's.

Obviously there will be places with prices that far exceed those numbers, but for a more middle-of-the-road type scenario, these are sufficient, and sufficient enough to substantially increase your tips. You will need to do a little homework here, but I think you will find it interesting as well as enjoyable. It's also knowledge and a skill you can use to outwit your friends and family. It can be very impressive, while adding a lot more money to your weekly pay.

THE ABILITY TO READ
YOUR GUESTS

I would be doing you and your restaurant a disservice if I didn't spend some time on this issue. This is not a contradiction to the previous section, but simply a reinforcement of the proper way to initiate, and where to be cautious in order to ensure success. It is imperative that you don't approach every table in the exact same manner regarding selling. The one crucial point I must mention here is the ability to not "oversell" or push people that have very definite ideas about what they want (and don't want) during their visit with you. Please guard against seeming calculating or like you're reading from the company server sales book.

In order for sales techniques to be successful, they must come naturally. More importantly, you will encounter all sorts of people in all types of situations. You may get two men who are in a hurry and just want a quick bite and off they go, and therefore don't have time for chitchat and recommendations. You may encounter a couple that is having an argument and won't be receptive to anything, including small talk or suggestions. You may have a group sit at your table and everyone is on a fixed budget for that meal.

As you get more comfortable in distinguishing who's who, you will find that your chances for "successful suggestive selling" will increase exponentially. Reading a guest can't be taught, it's instinctive. You can, however, improve your instincts. Just by being aware of how important this aspect is, you've already improved your chances. Be observant at first, even at the risk of not selling more in the beginning. It's much more beneficial to proceed with caution, at first, and hone your sales skills for future successes.

However having said this, done with sincerity and skill, suggestive selling will enhance the dining experience for your guests. As long as you don't give the guest a sense that you're trying to "pump up" their check needlessly or to make a quick buck that day. Be sure not to seem insincere, shallow or manipulative. When it is beneficial to your guests, it will naturally be of benefit to you.

So, if your manager is pushing you to increase your average covers, he may not have the best long-term interests for you or the restaurant in mind. Contests are great and most often a lot of fun. Just go about your business with the genuine care of your guests in mind. Their happiness and satisfaction is the bottom line and also what will drive your sales revenues long term for you and the restaurant.

Asking the Right Questions

The most talented people in sales realize that success comes down to a simple skill: Asking the right questions of the prospective customer. By asking the right questions, you can lead your guests to the best choices regarding your particular menu. Well, in your case, once the customer sits at your table, they're no longer a prospect, but indeed your customer.

We still, however, need to sell some items, and we will still accomplish this by merely asking the right questions. We also want to seem like we're recommending, not selling. We don't want to give the impression that we are just trying to run up their tab. We are simply trying to help our guest get the most out of their dining experience with us. Here are a few examples of questions and suggestive statements that you can use everyday. Try not to ask closed questions (where "no" can be an answer). It's always a choice of something, or something else, not something or nothing. Tailor them to your own comfort level and pick one or two to start with that you are completely comfortable with. Then build from there.

1. Would you care for still or sparkling water for the table?

2. Do you prefer a cocktail OR glass of wine to start while you're looking over your menu?

3. Would anyone care to try one of our new (pick a specialty drink you really like)?

4. If you would like to try something different, please look at our specialty drink menu for some great suggestions.

5. Would you like to order an appetizer while deciding on your entrees?

6. There are a couple of appetizers that are absolutely fantastic that you should consider if you never tried them before …

7. Would you care for soup, OR salad before your entrée?

8. The portions are generous/large here; perhaps you may just want to split an appetizer.

9. I've brought a wine list, so you may choose a wine with your dinner, if you're interested.

10. (If a couple or table of guests orders glasses of wine) If you think you may have more than one glass of wine, you may want to consider purchasing a bottle which will be a much better value for you.

11. (If no sides or accompaniments are offered with your entrée) would you prefer our fresh vegetable OR chef's potato to go along with that?

12. Would you like a side of pasta OR a fresh vegetable with that?

13. Would anyone care for some warm garlic bread?

14. May I bring you another cocktail (ask when glass is 2/3 empty)?

15. Please save some room for dessert, the chef has incredible specialties tonight (not a question but a good hint).

16. (With them in hand) I've brought dessert menus for everyone to look at (bring out dessert tray or cart if available). For those who won't order a large dessert, suggest a small ice cream or sherbet.

17. Do you prefer coffee or cappuccino? (During cold weather especially) Always suggest two specialty coffees and even a hot chocolate with peppermint schnapps in addition to typical after dinner drinks.

Even if selling makes you nervous, these are merely suggestions to increase your checks. Your guest's comfort level with this is directly proportionate to your own. The better you are, the more at ease they will be.

Pay Attention to the Entertainer

This is always an incredible opportunity, as long as you don't seem like you're taking advantage. Watch for the man or woman who seems to be picking up the check. If this is a celebration or reward of any kind, you just got lucky. This is where *reading* your guest becomes so important. Your communication is only as good as your understanding of the person you're communicating with. Cater to everyone naturally, but pay special attention to this person.

This person may be entertaining guests for a number of reasons including a reward for some business success they've recently enjoyed. In this case, nothing is too good for my people (who have probably made him or her look very good in the eyes of the boss and/or stockholders of the company). In this case, the boss wants to show his or her appreciation for the guests by thanking them with a night out. Does the boss care what they order? No! Is the boss going to monitor the size of the check? Probably not. Now it's time to really suggest. Everyone at this table should be having appetizers, salads, a cocktail while ordering, desserts, specialty coffees and after dinner drinks.

In all cases, remember to always guard against looking like you are trying to run up the bill unnecessarily to pad your tip. You are better off selling a bit less and earning a 25% tip, than getting only 15% on a slightly larger check. I know servers that will approach the person in charge to see if there are any parameters on ordering. The person in charge usually appreciates this and will respect you and the restaurant for this. Then, if they give you the green light, you can be comfortable in the selling role.

Remember when people go out to eat, they want a full course meal. Sometimes they can't afford this. But when someone else is treating, watch out. I've dined with people who can barely finish an entrée, until the company Christmas party and then they get an appetite like a grizzly bear. Strange isn't it? You need to be aware of this by reading the guests. And if you suspect a table is in this very situation, don't be afraid to make conversation to discover the nature of their night out. If someone at the table says 'the boss is treating us to dinner," you better put your selling hat on and make the most of the opportunity, without taking advantage of the host. Don't ever do anything to endanger your long term relationships.

If your average cover is normally $20 per person, this table should average $30 to $40 with no problem at all. And if you're really persuasive, $60 is not impossible. Three or four bottles of wine for the table will take care of most of that. You never want to gouge people, because you want them to return. And you may encounter people who will pull you aside and tell you there is some sort of limit on what they can spend. Make sure you follow those instructions and don't embarrass the host. But, with that said, if you're providing value and great service, you're not taking advantage, you're fulfilling a need or desire.

Vanity, another motivation in entertaining, is a whole different issue, but normally as easy to spot. This is the type of man who wants to show off for his guests. The guy sitting at the head of the table is saying, "Order anything you want" or "get my guests whatever they need". Your attitude should immediately say, "You got it!" You've seen them before and this is the perfect time to do exactly that. Get their guests anything they want!!!

Keep in mind that our business is no different from any other by the mere fact that it's a game of numbers and averages. One party like this can make your whole night, or even a week sometimes. Be wise, be professional, be charming and sell product. If you've gotten a couple bad tips, this can clearly make up for it.

You should also bring this man your wine list and ask if he would like to order some wine for his guests with dinner. Is he going to say no? Not likely. Remember he or she is here to thank all of the hard working employees who have helped him or her become successful, or to simply impress the guests. And don't think the people sitting at the table don't know and understand this. If you take care of this group, chances are very good they will come back again and again for other events and occasions.

Special Occasions

This is such a great time to make new friends, and lifelong customers. Just as I wrote about in the last section, these are oftentimes the best parties to serve. People out for birthdays, anniversaries and so on, are in the best of moods. You have the opportunity to not only create a wonderful experience for the host and their guests, but also create a profound memory for the guest of honor and all those who attend.

Don't' we always attach more meaning to what occurs during these very meaningful events? Doesn't an occasion seem to magnify the occurrences of the day? It is the perfect opportunity to make a great impression on a large group of people and develop some relationships that will last and grow into the future.

Having been fortunate enough to be very involved with catering large functions, including weddings, some of my best repeat guests are those who started with a banquet. I can honestly say, there is no appreciation you will ever experience from your guests as that of those who have enjoyed a significant milestone in your venue.

Always bear in mind that, even though we may see dozens and dozens of parties that celebrate all sorts of occasions, each one is unique and special to the people involved. Never trivialize the significance and always play it up big for the guest of honor, and the person who is hosting the event. Plus everyone who attends, and also enjoys it, will think of your place (and hopefully you in particular) when a similar event arises in their lives or that of their family and friends.

They will tell countless people who will then patronize your restaurant. This is how restaurants thrive and flourish. Special times generate special memories that last forever. That's the word I want you to remember here. Forever.

Don't Forget the Kids

If you work in a restaurant that features a children's menu, you have some great opportunities for "up selling" these little customers. I know most servers regard children as a "drag" on their average covers (no offense intended for the moms and dads, this is a business discussion). No matter what the average adult spends, the revenue generated through a child is often 50–70% less, and thereby substantially lessens, or "drags down" your tip at the end. So those of you who encounter eight or ten or even more children in a week's time need to be a bit creative in your sales approach to this audience, without hurting the parents or causing financial concern.

The very first thing you need to suggest to your manager is to have special drinks for kids. I did this in two locations that increased revenues through kids by 60%. Rather than the soda, milk and juices for about a dollar, we created frozen specialty drinks for the kids at four dollars each. They were listed right on the kid's menus, complete with descriptions.

They were flavors that had an extremely high appeal towards the kids, with ingredients that were easily approved by their parents because they were healthier than soda. It was a natural. Most times, you would never even have to mention this. The kids became your salesmen. THEY could get their parents to agree to one of these items more times than not. After all, what's four dollars compared to a lack of peace and quiet during dinner? It's only a four dollar item, but in reality, you've just quadrupled the sales for that child in beverages (not to mention if you could get a second ordered). However, should the kids miss it, by simply asking the parents if they would prefer a healthier drink choice for their children as opposed to soda, you've just opened the door to a larger tip with very little effort.

Without question, your check averages are brought down with children at the table. Their meals are three dollars, four dollars and five dollars depending on your restaurant and kid's menu, which seriously affects the final total of the bill. If you can increase these covers alone, perhaps to the point of doubling sales, you will naturally earn double the tips as well. Don't risk offending the parents. Many will dine out without the children and you want that also to be with you.

Now you may be thinking to yourself, that's not going to be any big deal, I don't wait on that many kids anyway. But even if your tips in one week are only $25 off children's sales, why not make them $50. It's still an extra $100 per month!

It's vital for you to remember that this is a business of many small gains on several points of focus. Add them all up, as you will see in the next section, and you will now be looking at hundreds of extra dollars.

Our success accumulates as we increase these smaller focal points until we have improved our income substantially across the board. As you read on, you will see this more plainly.

Let's Talk Money

Even though I tried to keep this information very concise, so as to make for easy reading, I know you're thinking, "This all sounds well and good, but how much money can I really make"? This is my favorite part of this book. This is what excited and motivated me enough to put all of this information together. So, without working harder, without picking up an extra shift, or working a double or waiting on one single extra guest, *This Is How YOU Make More Money*.

Let's assume that you work four shifts per week, which would consist of about 25 hours per week (the average server's work week as reported by the National Restaurant Association). Average covers vary greatly depending upon what type establishment you work in, but for this illustration, let's use an average cover of $20.00. I know some places will be only $10 or $15, but others can be $40 to $50 and well beyond (including **Per Se** in NYC whose average cover is $250 according to *Restaurants & Institutions* Top 100 Independent Restaurants). The percentage will always be the same, however.

For anyone thinking about getting into this business, your average cover is simply the amount of money each customer spends at any given time. An average cover is your total sales divided by the number of guests you served. $800 in sales with 25 guests served = a $32 average cover. So with $20 as the example, a typical party of four guests would have a check of $80.

Using this formula, and assuming you are making the "traditional" tip of 15%, this is what your income would be for a typical month (plus your paycheck).

Example	# Covers	Avg Cover	Shifts/Week	Total Sales	x 15%	x 4 Weeks	Difference
1	20	$20.00	4	$1,600	$240	$960	—

In example #1 you are making $960 per month in tips. Perhaps you think this is okay for a part-time job four days a week. After all, maybe the goal was just to make a couple extra dollars each week for some "mad" money. As long as you are working at this particular eating establishment, anyway, you might as well try to take a couple more dollars home with you. Let's look at how quickly this changes with some points of focus. Let's see how dramatically this can change by focusing on sales first. Remember, you control this. You don't need to wait for a raise; you can earn more on your next shift!

Example	# Covers	Avg Cover	Shifts/Week	Total Sales	x 15%	x 4 Weeks	Difference
2	20	$23.00	4	$1,840	$276	$1,104	$144.00
3	20	$26.00	4	$2,080	$312	$1,248	$288.00
4	20	$30.00	4	$2,400	$360	$1,440	$480.00

The previous example illustrates how a small increase in your average cover over example #1, will substantially increase your monthly income. We're still making only 15% tips on our checks. Example # 2 can be achieved easily with an extra soda, cup of soup, small salad, side of fries or vegetables, baked potato or maybe a scoop of ice cream, rice pudding or piece of pie. Or, one technique that has tremendous success is suggesting a couple "split" an appetizer or dessert. This helps solve the problem of the couple who is both watching their spending as well as those watching their calories. After all, what could only "half" of something hurt?"

This is as good a time as any to emphasize dessert sales. It would be negligent if I didn't spend some time on this area. Everyone wants dessert! Everyone. Assume this every time people finish dinner. The issue is that many people have different reasons for denying it, but they still want it. Use separate dessert menus, use trays or carts to show these after dinner treats to your guests. Seeing is believing when it comes to desserts. Who can resist an incredible looking piece of dessert? If you have faith in your product, this is going to be a no-brainer.

If you work in a place that features nice selections, your goal should be to increase your average covers by 20% alone on dessert sales. Worst case scenario, get a couple to split a dessert. Even if I know I shouldn't order a dessert because I'm too full or I can't afford the calories or I've already had one sweet today, or whatever, I will order a dessert if it looks good enough, just to have a bite or two. Make it a goal that every couple, on average, will at least split a dessert and you will easily be in example #2 (or higher) which is $144 more in earnings. Just by one recommendation, that's all. If you do this, you will realize more success.

If you make the item, any item, sound like they **have to** try it if they never have before, you will find success. And let us not forget that premium wine, or asking which particular liquor the guest prefers ($1 to $12 additional charge) is constantly adding to your total sales. It also helps to offer bottled sparkling or still water when you first approach the table. Many people prefer it to the water taken from the tap, although don't ask them in this fashion, just offer the bottled.

Example # 3 can be achieved with an appetizer, bowl of soup, dessert, a second cocktail, glass of wine with dinner or an after dinner drink. # 4 takes one specialty drink, premium glass of wine, a bottle of wine at the table (or better yet that second bottle of wine), appetizers, desserts, adding a potato and vegetable to an entrée, cappuccino, after dinner cordials, etc. It isn't as hard as you think. Once you get into the habit of suggesting, you will become comfortable with selling. It will occur automatically and become something you do subconsciously without any fear or concern.

I currently work with a young lady who is a server for the first time in her life. She reads the same materials you are and oftentimes she beats other more experienced servers in average covers. Maybe it's because she brings no fears or misconceptions about selling. Everything she says and does is simply a matter of fact and done with the utmost sincerity. I marvel at how much money she makes. She has quit her retail job to pursue this fulltime and will tell you she has never made more money before. And she's still learning everyday how to get better.

To be conservative and because menus differ as do results, depending upon where you live and work, let's use the middle example, #3 in measuring our additional income on a monthly basis. With an extra $288 per month as shown in the chart over example #1, we just paid one or two utility bills or did our shopping for one week (depending on family size and appetite). Remember, this is found money. We're not working any additional days to earn this.

The following chart is for those who feel they can't possibly sell because it's too pushy or even rude. I disagree, but it wouldn't be the first time I heard this. So the next chart (examples 5–8) will illustrate how we improve our tips, not by increasing our sales, but by the average amount of a tip our guests leave us.

Example	# Covers	Avg Cover	Shifts/Week	Total Sales	x 18%	x 4 Weeks	Difference
5	20	$20.00	4	$1,600	$288	$1,152	$192.00
6	20	$23.00	4	$1,840	$331	$1,325	$365.00
7	20	$26.00	4	$2,080	$374	$1,498	$538.00
8	20	$30.00	4	$2,400	$432	$1,728	$768.00

Now let's look to example #5. We were so shy that we didn't sell anything additional. Not one of our guests took any of our suggestions. Our tables didn't drink and didn't want any appetizers. Just like in example #1. The key here is, we were a little nicer, smiled more or were just a bit more prompt in our service. So we earned 18% instead of 15% and earned an extra $192 for our efforts. What would $192 per month pay for you? Not bad right, but there's so much more we're leaving out here.

I want you to really think about this. How hard would it be to sell a cup of soup or salad? Would it be so terrible if you told the guest about the apple cobbler your restaurant is famous for or a nice specialty coffee on a cold winter's day, or even a non-alcohol frozen drink instead of a soda?

We know this is pretty easy. And since we know this, being a little more attentive will earn us more money. Our guests gave us the same 18% as in #5, but we've now moved up just slightly into #6. Because of this, we've now we've earned an additional $365 for the month. Don't look now, but I think we've got a modest car payment all of a sudden. $365 for selling a soup and being nice? Seems far too easy, doesn't it? There must be something wrong here. Read on. Now it's getting interesting.

If we can do this, then #7 is also within our grasp. After all, what do we need to do? Sell that appetizer, or maybe have the table split a couple appetizers if they feel that one each is too expensive. How about a dessert, specialty coffee, or glass of wine with dinner? I know I'm being repetitious but the more you read this, the more it will become second nature to you. You've only added $6 to the average cover. It's not a huge sum of money, is it? If you agree, you just added about $538 more in your wallet at the end of the month? Now we can pay several utility bills or a payment on a nicer car or half a month's rent or a mortgage, maybe???

Don't Leave Money on the Table

Now you're asking the right questions, selling more and executing well. Your check averages are already higher. I've discussed being courteous and polite. Let's really try to increase the percentage of tip we can earn by being nice and motivating people to like you. Let's be worthy of that extra 3, 5 or even 10% on our checks.

We have all been to restaurants and experienced a very pleasant server. These types of servers don't really spend any extra time with us, but all of the times they do come over to our table, they are upbeat and pleasant. They smile and greet everyone at the table with just a quick, but not rushed, glance. They are able to detect if we need anything at anytime by paying attention to the table, while not constantly walking over and interrupting us with, "Is everything okay?" They simply stroll by and make eye contact and, in the event we need them, we know they are near and easily accessible.

And doesn't this make a huge difference in our dining experience? Aren't you more likely to forgive a service error or overlook a mistake because of their personality? If the food is average, but the service is excellent, don't you regard the experience as a good one? By the time you leave, you now feel a sort of bond with this individual that you only met an hour or two earlier. And how many times has someone in your group said, "The next time we come here, I'm going to ask to be sat in his/her station again." To me, this is always worth an extra 5–10% tip every time and without fail.

But let's be conservative. Let's look at it on a smaller scale. For argument's sake, add only 3% and see what the difference is:

Example	# Covers	Avg Cover	Shifts/Week	Total Sales	x 21%	x 4 Weeks	Difference
9	20	$26.00	4	$2,080	$436	$1,1747	$787.00

Now if it's a car payment we're looking for, what kind could you buy with an extra $787 a month? The example we're talking about now is only a 21% tip. A lot of people will leave this much automatically if they like the service. In fact, most people today use 20% as a guide for a minimum tip for good service. People who really enjoy their service will tip 25–30% without thinking twice.

Now when you feel you can really sell, and know you can charm your guests, look at example #10.

Example	# Covers	Avg Cover	Shifts/Week	Total Sales	x 21%	x 4 Weeks	Difference
10	20	$30.00	4	$2,400	$504	$2,016	$1,056.00

Now we've paid, or at least almost paid, our rent or mortgage for the month. What? Did I write this correctly? You brought home a mere $1,056.00 EXTRA for the month? Yes, you did! Remember, many people who are impressed with your service, professionalism and personality will tip 25% and more. So assume that you can be nicer than ever. Modestly put, you're going to get everyone of your guests to love you. And when you figure out how to increase your sales—Look at #11!

Example	# Covers	Avg Cover	Shifts/Week	Total Sales	x 25%	x 4 Weeks	Difference
11	20	$30.00	4	$2,400	$600	$2,400	$1,440.00

You just paid your *mortgage* without picking up that second job, working all the holidays or volunteering to do double shifts. Not only have you not worked a moment longer, but you haven't worked any harder. You're still working only four shifts per week. So how did you do it?

You smiled. You were nice. You were gracious. You were engaging. You made conversation. You were confident and competent. You're already all these things or you wouldn't be in this business for any length of time. You helped your guests by confidently suggesting items. You were prepared with several recommendations every time you went to a table. You let everyone know just how good various menu items and drink specials were. You were simply working more efficiently at your job and focusing on the points of service and selling.

You're working the same job, the same number of days, and the same number of hours and just gave yourself a 150% raise!!!

Remember the $960 you were making originally? Now you're making $2,400 in the same period of time. You didn't have to wait for your boss to give it to you. You gave it to yourself. This is completely in YOUR control.

No matter who you are, what your personality or even confidence level is, there is a number on one of the previous charts for you. We can all be nicer, sell more or both. No matter what your nature, one way or another, you can and will increase your income. Give yourself a chance and start slowly by simply being nicer and more efficient. Add the sales in, as time passes, and you will become more and more comfortable. It will all seem very natural and begin to get easier everyday.

Product Knowledge

Politeness, courtesy and a warm smile will not make up for incompetence. There are a lot of very pleasant people walking around that can't get out of their own way. So we need to be very good at what we do. But since you have chosen this line of work, it would logically follow that you want to be the best you can. If this is not your feeling, you should find another line of work, immediately.

You MUST know your menu and drinks. You MUST know enough of your wine list to make quick and accurate recommendations. I cannot emphasize wines enough to you. They can be extremely influential in your sales efforts. Be able to describe them to the guest in a way that "sells" them on your suggestions. Accurate knowledge and confidence in one's products helps the sale.

No one pays attention to a person who is unsure about that which they are speaking. You must be poised and confident at all times. Isn't it a little frustrating when you're dining out and ask a server about something on the menu, and they say they'll have to find out first? This is a simple case of not knowing your business, and that's going to negatively impact your guests' experience and consequently, your earning potential.

So now, when you first approach the table, you're ready with suggestions and answers about your specialty drinks. So now, we simply need to find out what type of drink. When you approach the table, you simply ask, "Would you care for a cocktail or glass of wine before dinner?" It's always a choice of something or something else. This is the time to suggest a specialty drink or martini since they are $7 and $8 each ($14 to $19 in NYC). For those non-drinkers, we have non-alcohol frozen specialty drinks or bottled water. If they are just going to have water, they'll have to earn that right by turning down everything.

It's also critical to remember that when a guest says no to you, don't take it personally. Restaurant people tend to, and need to have thick skin. Keep in mind that it's people's nature to spend money. Who doesn't enjoy this? Our job is to get them to spend it here, with us, at our table! You're only helping them do what they came to do.

For those who work in country clubs or any private club, you already have a captive audience. You don't have to worry about getting people in the doors. And right now, you may feel that the members won't tip the way I suggested previously. If this is true, it's only because they have never been served the way you will serve them now. Good service will bring good tips.

You are already in the very fortunate position of being guaranteed a certain percentage on every check in many clubs. Please do not regard this as **not** having to go the "extra mile" for your guests. Nothing could be farther from the truth. The members will expect it, and your managers and supervisors will demand it. You are in a performance-based job and will be judged every shift you work.

When I took over managing a private club, I increased the automatic gratuity placed on all members' bills from 15 to 18%. This was not very popular with the members initially. We had to work very hard to prove the staff was worth it. But in a few short months, the new staff I hired was up to speed and outperforming the previous employees.

Now the staff could have said they got a raise and had been happy, which may have been atypical for one of my staffs because I made their earnings an intricate part of all conversations. Most every server will earn additional tips now because of their attitude and service. They are not satisfied with 18%. They want 20 and 25% tips each shift. And this happens more often than not.

Good tips need to further motivate us rather than make us complacent. All you need to do is change a habit or two in your work life to realize what's been described. Take a couple extra seconds at your table to listen to your guests, help them with suggestions, and execute your duties to the best of your abilities. Treat the guests as if they were in your home. You are there to serve them graciously and professionally, not as if they are inconveniencing you. You will find extra money in your paycheck and probably have a better time while you're at work as well.

Repeat Customers
~ Reap the Rewards

Remember when we talked about "passion" in a previous section? That's a huge part of what brings people not only back to our restaurant, but right back into our section. This is *your* business remember. Not unlike a hairdresser that counts on customers coming back again and again. We also want to build a "following." Bartenders often do this with great success. We have to excel at our job in order to create a need or a desire for our services. Even if you don't increase your average covers, but you do such a great job that you consistently get guests to come back, you will make more money! You will do so through increasing volume and becoming an effective marketing tool. I call this a reward because you have to do a good job during a guest's first visit in order for them to return. Now that they're back, you have increased revenues for your restaurant and put yourself in a position to prosper, as you will see.

When you get a repeat customer back to see you, chances are you're already in a position to earn 5–15% more right off the bat. Look back the examples I illustrated and you will see that a mere 6% is worth

$600 a month more in our pocket. You need repeat customers. And the only way you are going to acquire this is by standing out, delivering great service and suggesting all the great specials and items your restaurant is offering that day, which is also the way you build you sales and average covers.

An important note here is that these are also the guests who will be more receptive to your suggestive selling. You've already established some sort of bond, which means there is more trust between you both. You usually will have a little more latitude in these cases, and therefore have the ability to help influence certain decisions on their parts.

Never be too presumptuous, always remain professional, but use the relationship you've established to enhance their experience even more. People like to be fawned over, especially in front of their guests. Use all the charms you did to bring them back initially.

This is huge and I purposely saved it for the end to be sure it sticks in your mind. You are leaving a lot of money behind if you never get people to come back and see you. All successful companies and businesses rely on repeat customers. You're helping your restaurant, coworkers and yourself all at the same time.

Remember the woman I described earlier who was driving a Mercedes in less than a year? She never even considered herself a good salesperson. Her strength was in the amount of average tip she generated. She concentrated on her people skills and, all of a sudden, she went from averaging 18% to 25% all the time! She knew her forte was in getting people to like her, and she made the most of it. That's why you don't have to be a great salesperson to earn more money in this business.

Look back at example #1, where you were earning 15% on sales with an average cover of $20. If you also feel that sales are not your strong point or you're uncomfortable suggesting items to guests, increase your tips to 25% on those sales and you're now earning $1,600 a month as opposed to $960. That's a 60% raise in tips for the same amount of sales! That's why, no matter what your personality type, you can accomplish your goals through sales or better service or both. There's a way for every single server to succeed.

Don't Relax When Things are Going Well

Sometimes human nature dictates that we ease up when things are going well. I heard Tony Robbins say once, "When things are good, we celebrate. When they're bad, we contemplate." I want to caution you on your success, so you can keep it going.

I have seen it over and over again and have been guilty of it myself. We tend to step back and marvel at what we've done; a little self-admiration perhaps. But right then, that very second, whether we feel it or not, we're in danger of letting complacency slip in. We have to guard against feeling like, "This is it! We've finally succeeded!" You see it in sports. One team is winning by a large margin, gets cocky and complacent, and all of a sudden, the other team comes back and is now winning. We start to get caught up in our own success and begin to lose sight of things at hand, and maybe even the long-term goal we set out to accomplish.

It's when things are going well that we have to focus, even more intently, on what we're doing in order for our prosperity to continue. It's much easier to succeed initially than it is to maintain it. In hospitality, **Complacency Kills**. Remember that phrase because you can drive down any Main Street in America and see a closed up building that used to be a good restaurant. And everybody always asks the same thing, "I wonder what happened?"

Now I don't mean to suggest that this is the cause of failure in every case. Sometimes it's terrible food, poor financial management, unsanitary conditions and several other possibilities. But if you're in a good location that is clean and fairly attractive with decent to good food and honest ownership, it will be complacency on the part of the managers and front of house staff more times than not.

So take time and appreciate what you've accomplished. Be proud of the great strides you will soon see in your work life. But don't dwell on the past. Build on it. Improve on what you did yesterday in order to keep building on your successes. It's fine to stop along the path and admire the scenery, but you need to continue the journey.

There's a quote from author Harold Melcher in which he writes, "Live your life each day as you would climb a mountain. An occasional glance towards the summit keeps the goal in mind, but many beautiful scenes are to be observed from each new vantage point. Climb slowly, steadily, enjoying each passing moment; and the view from the summit will serve as a fitting climax for the journey."

The other element I would like you to consider is to lift those around you as you climb. Bring someone up along with you. Help elevate them. This, I believe, is our most important purpose in life, professionally or personally. To make a difference in another person's life is the way we give back to those who helped us along the way. This is Karma.

Your First
Responsibility

I know it's a strange place to put this section. It seems like it should have been the introductory section you read. We've discussed many things in this book, but I want to be certain that this stays with you above all else.

Any restaurant is a service-oriented business. This means that *Job One* is to be sure our guests are happy. If they aren't, you and your restaurant are in big trouble. It won't matter what your average check or tips are, you'll be in an empty building eventually.

Consider this: If everyone who eats in your restaurant was so happy that they told two of their friends and couldn't wait to return, how much better would you business be for everyone? I suggest to you that the amount of business you will do is inconceivable if you just make certain your guests are happy. If the first impression you make is anything other than trying to please the guests, it will catch up with you in a negative way.

That's why I described, at length, both your ability to sell as well as the ability to get your guests to like you. You can earn more money with both. And you can start with endearing yourself to your guests in order to raise the percentage of your average tips. You still benefit your company by this and don't ever let anyone tell you any different. Treat people like YOU would like to be treated. Use this as your measuring stick and you'll never go wrong. Your guests represent your income, and it's so crucial you keep this in mind. Our success is truly dependent upon the lengths in which we are willing to go to take care of our guests. Just look at the following chart for some facts regarding our guests:

*

Some Startling Facts Regarding the Reasons Businesses Lose Customers

Customer Dies	1%
Moved Away	3%
Influenced by Friends	5%
Lured Away by the Competition	9%
Dissatisfied with Product	14%
Turned Away by the Attitude of Indifference On the Part of the Company Employee	68%

*   Source: THE PRYOR REPORT, Vol 10, No. 4a

Follow Through

I hope you have found this book to be a useful tool and an effective way to start earning more money immediately. It will only be of value to you if you follow through. And unlike many books that suggest you alter your life completely, I only suggest you place your attention on two small facets of your work. You don't need to take any educational courses, work 15 more hours from home, sell things to your friends, or any of the other ideas out there that promise to make you more money. Just focus on what you do, and do it the best you can and you will succeed. Just do the following:

1. Suggest those items that are sure to please your guests.

2. Be nicer to your guests than anyone.

This is all you need to do. You will find that if you consciously think about your sales everyday, just from the mere fact that you are placing your attention on this element of your job, your performance will automatically improve just because of your awareness. Anything we place our attention on generally improves. Things we pay little or no attention to usually suffer. We can find evidence of this in both our personal and professional lives.

So many times, we wait for others or other circumstances that could improve our lot in life. Now you can earn more money for you starting with your very next shift. Everything you've read here you can immediately apply, and if you follow through, you will see the rewards instantly. Not next month or next year, but this week.

Look at your sales everyday. Critique your performance on a daily basis and you cannot help but improve. What was it you wanted that extra money for again? Write down on your pad you will now bring to work with you, in big, bold letters, your dream; your goal. Use a picture to give you a more compelling visual; car, college, vacation, condo, house, or whatever you want to give yourself and your family in the near future. This way every time you begin a shift, you will have a great source of motivation at your fingertips.

Any time you wish to positively change something, the first thing you must do is raise your standards. Don't settle for status quo. If you want better, you must change. The thing we can always control is our own actions. This is usually more than enough for us to become successful. Use this as a roadmap to help you get to your desired goal.

If you keep doing what you've always done, you will keep getting what you've always gotten. Jack Welch of GE prominence once said, "Control your destiny, or someone else will." You need to shape your life and yourself. Give yourself that raise starting today because you have earned it!

978-0-595-46917-8
0-595-46917-5

www.ingramcontent.com/pod-product-compliance
Lightning Source LLC
Chambersburg PA
CBHW030813180526
45163CB00003B/1262